9th Joint ISO – ACL SIGSEM Workshop on Interoperable Semantic Annotation 2013

Held at the 10th International Conference on Computational Semantics (IWCS 2013)

Potsdam, Germany
19 March 2013

Editors:

Harry Bunt

ISBN: 978-1-62748-399-5

Printed from e-media with permission by:

Curran Associates, Inc.
57 Morehouse Lane
Red Hook, NY 12571

Some format issues inherent in the e-media version may also appear in this print version.

Printed by Curran Associates, Inc. (2013)

For permission requests, please contact the Association for Computational Linguistics at the address below.

Association for Computational Linguistics
209 N. Eighth Street
Stroudsburg, Pennsylvania 18360

Phone: 1-570-476-8006
Fax: 1-570-476-0860

acl@aclweb.org

Additional copies of this publication are available from:

Curran Associates, Inc.
57 Morehouse Lane
Red Hook, NY 12571 USA
Phone: 845-758-0400
Fax: 845-758-2634
Email: curran@proceedings.com
Web: www.proceedings.com

Proceedings of the 9th Joint ISO - ACL SIGSEM Workshop on Interoperable Semantic Annotation

isa-9

March 19–20, 2013

Potsdam, Germany

Harry Bunt, editor

Table of Contents:

Preface

This slender volume contains the accepted long and short papers that were submitted to the 9th Joint ISO-ACL/SIGSEM Workshop on Interoperable Semantic Annotation, isa-9, which was organized in at the University of Potsdam, in the historical city of Potsdam, Germany, March 19-20, 2013.

isa-9 is the ninth edition of joint workshops on the International Organization for Standards ISO and the ACL Special Interest Group in Computational Semantics, Working Group "The Representation of Multimodal Semantic Information (`http://sigsem.uvt.nl`). The main focus of these workshops is on the presentation and discussion of approaches, experiments, experiences, and proposals concerning the construction or application of interoperable linguistic resources with semantic annotations. The isa workshops are often organized on the occasion of meetings of ISO projects concerned with the establishment of international standards for semantic annotation and representation, or as a workshop of a larger conference that is dedicated to related issues. For ISA-9 the occasion is the 10th International Conference on Computational Semantics IWCS 2013, and as such the workshop traces the footsteps of ISA workshops that were held in Tilburg in 2005, 2007, and 2009, and in Oxford in 2011, on the occasion of the IWCS 2005, 2007, 2009, and 2011 conferences.

The isa-9 workshop co-includes meetings of several subprojects of the ISO project 24617, "Semantic annotation framework (SemAF)", in particular of those concerned with the annotation of spatial information, the annotation of semantic roles, the annotation of discourse relations, and basic issues in semantic annotation.

I would like to thank the members of the isa-9 Programme Committee for their careful and quick reviewing, and the organizers of the the IWCS 2013 conference for supporting the organization of isa-9 as an IWCS 2013 workshop.

Harry Bunt
isa-8 chair

Programme Committee:

Jan Alexandersson
Collin Baker
Harry Bunt (chair)
Nicoletta Calzolari
Jae-Woong Choe
Thierry Declerck
Alex C. Fang
Robert Gaizauskas
Koti Hasida
Nancy Ide
Aravind Joshi
Michael Kipp
Kiyong Lee
Inderjeet Mani
Martha Palmer
Volha Petukhova
Massimo Poesio
Andrei Popescu-Belis
Rashmi Prasad
James Pustejovsky
Laurent Romary
Ted Sanders
Thorsten Trippel
Piek Vossen
Annie Zaenen

Organizing Committee:

Harry Bunt (Tiburg University)
Kiyong Lee (Korea University, Seoul)
James Pustejovsky (Brandeis University, Waldham, MA)
Laurent Romary (CNRS, Berlin)

9th Joint ACL-ISO Workshop on Interoperable Semantic Annotation

Workshop Programme

Tuesday, March 19, 2013

University of Potsdam, Griebnitzsee Campus, Building 6, Room 23

08:45 - 09:15	On-site registration
09:15 - 09:20	Welcome, opening
09:20 - 09:55	Caterina Mauri, Malvina Nissim, Paola Pietrandrea & Andrea Sanso: *Which units for modality annotation?*
09:55 - 10:30	Kiyong Lee: *Multi-layered annotation of non-textual data for spatial information*
10:30 - 11:00	coffee break
11:00 - 11:35	James Pustejovsky: *Capturing motion in ISO-SpaceBank*
11:35 - 12:30	Overview and Status Report of Project ISO-Space (James Pustejovsky)
	lunch break
14:00 - 14:25	Steve Cassidy: *Interoperability in the Australian National Corpus*
14:25 - 15:00	Harry Bunt & Martha Palmer: *Conceptual and representational choices in defining an ISO standard for semantic role annotation*
15:00 - 15:30	Overview and Status Report of ISO-Semantic Roles (Harry Bunt)
15:30 - 16:00	tea break
16:00 - 16:30	Annie Zaenen & Lauri Karttunen: *Veridicity annotation in the lexicon? A look at factive adjectives*
16:30 - 17:00	discussion on possible ISO project on veridicity annotation (Annie Zaenen)

Wednesday 20 March:
University of Potsdam, Griebnitzsee Campus, Building 6, Room 23

08:30 - 09:00	On-site IWCS 2013 Registration
09:00 - 10:00	IWCS 2013 invited talk by Manfred Pinkal
10:05 - 10:40	Ben Verhoeven & Gerard B. van Huyssteee: *More than only noun-noun compounds: Towards and annotation scheme for the semantic modeling of other noun compound terms*
10:40 - 11:10	coffee break
11:10 - 11:45	Harry Bunt, Alex Fang, Jin Cao, Xiaoyue Liu & Volha Petukhova: *Issues in the addition of ISO-compliant annotations to the Switchboard corpus*
11:45 - 12:15	Overview and Status Report of Project ISO-DRel (Semantic Relations in Discourse) (Rashmi Prasad)
	lunch break
14:00 - 14:30	Overview and Status Report of Project ISO-Basics (Harry Bunt)
14:30 - 14:55	Takenobu Tokunaga, Ryu Iida & Koh Mitsuda: *Annotation for annotation - Toward eliciting implicit linguistic knowledge through annotation*
14:55 - 15:30	James Pustejovsky: *Inference patterns with intensional adjectives*
15:30 - 16:00	tea break
16:00 - 16:45	Interoperability of ISO semantic annotation frameworks, either published or under development (Harry Bunt, Kiyong Lee, James Pustejovsky, Laurent Romary)
16:45 - 16:50	Workshop closing
16:50 - 17:30	ISO TC 37/SC 4 WGs plenary meeting

Cross-linguistic annotation of modality: a data-driven hierarchical model

Malvina Nissim
University of Bologna

Paola Pietrandrea
Lattice-CNRS, France

Andrea Sansò
University of Insubria

Caterina Mauri
University of Pavia

Abstract

We present an annotation model of modality which is (i) cross-linguistic, relying on a wide, strongly typologically motivated approach, and (ii) hierarchical and layered, accounting for both *factuality* and *speaker's attitude*, while modelling these two aspects through separate annotation schemes. Modality is defined through cross-linguistic categories, but the classification of actual linguistic expressions is language-specific. This makes our annotation model a powerful tool for investigating linguistic diversity in the field of modality on the basis of real language data, being thus also useful from the perspective of machine translation systems.

1 Introduction and Background

A text cannot be simply regarded as a sequence of representations of State of Affairs (SoAs) occurring (or having occurred) in the actual world. Texts may comprise representations of counterfactual or non factual SoAs, as well as a number of expressions encoding the stance the writer/speaker might be taking on a SoA, implying different attitudes, possibly relying on external sources of information. These aspects fall under the more general label of *modality*.

The automatic interpretation of modality can be seen as two tasks: (i) identifying the representations that are not put forward as factual and (ii) identifying the sentiments or opinions speakers may have towards their representations. These two tasks, which we call *factuality mining* and *speaker's attitude mining*, respectively, are two independent, albeit often related, semantic and linguistic dimensions.

Since the first step towards developing systems which deal with modality automatically is the creation of appropriate, annotated resources, the last few years have witnessed the development of annotation schemes and annotated corpora for different aspects of modality in different languages (McShane et al. (2004); Wiebe et al. (2005); Szarvas et al. (2008); Sauri and Pustejovsky (2009); Hendrickx et al. (2012); Baker et al. (2012)).

While important contributions, these remain mainly separate efforts. And while there have been efforts towards finding a common avenue for modality annotation, such as the CoNLL-2010 Shared Task, ACL thematic workshops and a special issue of Computational Linguistics (Morante and Sporleder (2012)), the computational linguistics community is still far from having developed working, shared standards for converting modality-related issues into annotation categories.

Linguistic theory, and especially linguistic typology, has already gone a long way in the study of modality across languages. However, this very aspect of cross-linguality has been overlooked in devising annotation schemes. Instead, we believe that working in a multilingual environment could ease the annotation, and at the same time make it more semantically meaningful, by keeping the layer of functional categories distinct from their actual linguistic realisations. Indeed, modality can be modelled more elegantly and efficiently starting from a functional, higher, level, while languages encode with their own means the specified concepts and categories.

Therefore, we promote an annotation model of modality which is (i) cross-linguistic, relying on a wide, strongly typologically motivated approach, (ii) adaptable, capable of accounting for the linguistic realisation of modality in each single language under consideration; and (iii) hierarchical and layered, accounting for both *factuality* and *speaker's attitude*, while modelling these two aspects through separate annotation schemes. Within this frame, the issue of *annotation units*, linguistically, becomes crucial, and we claim that such a two-layered framework provides the best setting for dealing with it.

2 Annotating Modality

In spite of the large amount of solid work on modality in theoretical linguistics and linguistic typology, and in spite of the various more NLP-oriented annotation schemes that are flourishing in the last years, there are as yet no shared standards for modality annotation. This is extreme to the point that Vincze et al. (2010) have observed, through a very detailed analysis and classification of problematic issues, that the same biomedical data was annotated in two different projects yielding minimal overlap, both semantically and syntactically.

A main issue is that there is no actual consensus on the very **notion of modality** to be translated into annotation categories. While it is *factuality* the key notion in Sauri and Pustejovsky (2009)'s FactBank, for instance, it is instead the *speaker's attitude* that is addressed in other recent annotation exercises (Nirenburg and McShane (2008); Hendrickx et al. (2012); Baker et al. (2012)).

Also not uniform across different projects is the actual **annotation procedure**, in terms of which functional categories must be annotated in text. It is quite common to consider the trigger, the scope, and the source (or author) as relevant categories, but not all of them translate into actual annotation. For example, in (Baker et al. (2010)), all three of them are signalled to the annotators in text, but it is only the targets which are to receive an annotation value.

And crucially, there are wide differences, and often little clarity, in terms of which **linguistic units** should be annotated. It has been shown in typological and constructional studies on modality that modal triggers may vary in nature and complexity (morphemes, verbs, adverbs, complex constructions, etc.) and that the scope of a modal marker may vary in extension from a single word to an entire text Masini and Pietrandrea (2010). One major problem is that in a few projects the annotators are not asked to select the annotation units but only to assign modality values to preselected markables, thus turning annotation into a classification task. In their annotation guidelines, Baker et al. (2010) assume that the units to be marked up are already highlighted and do not exceed the clause limit (i.e. the maximum extension is a phrase) and revolve around a verb, but it isn't clearly specified how such units are selected, nor why. Differently, Hendrickx et al. (2012) let the annotators choose the unit and its extension, allowing also for cross-sentential markables to be selected. However, they pre-select data to be annotated by matching a finite set of modality trigging verbs, thereby also imposing some degree of constraint. While pre-selecting annotation units maximises homogeinity and reduces disagreement among annotators, it is not clear exactly *which* units are to be marked up and whether it is at all an appropriate procedure in all cases.

Building on insights coming from linguistic typology, we will take a stand on these issues and claim that a cross-linguistic perspective provides the best framework for devising an annotation model for modality. We will also claim that the issue of annotation units must be addressed, and it becomes more meaningful and better dealt with within such a framework, thanks to a division between a *functional annotation*, where functional categories are specified and a *linguistic annotation* where actual units are selected for annotation, depending on the language. In Section 5 we will show how we suggest to combine these two different annotations.

3 A two-layered approach

Two related but distinct phenomena are often lumped together under the label of modality: factuality and speaker's attitude.

Factuality A representation can be put forward as depicting an event actually occurring or having occurred (factual SoAs, 1a), an event having not occurred in the real world (counterfactual SoAs, 1b), or not grounded in reality (non factual SoAs, 1c):

(1) a. He came

b. He did not come

c. She fears he came

As the examples show, the representation as such does not encode the factuality of the depicted event. It is only the context that allows for a specification of this value.

Speaker's attitude Speaker's attitude may also contribute to specify the factuality of a SoAs, but it does so only incidentally. The main purpose of the markers of speaker's attitude is specifying the stance of the speaker towards his representation, rather than the factuality status of that representation. The speaker can express his commitment about the SoA (epistemic modality), whether expressing his genuine commitment (commitment) or specifying the evidence he has for his opinion (evidential epistemic); he can can manifests his will concerning the SoA (deontic modality), whether expressing a mere wish (volitional deontic) or manipulating the adressee toward the realisation of the SoA (manipulative deontic); he can express his moral or esthetic judgment about a SoA or his fear about it (evaluative modality).

Two orthogonal dimensions Sometimes the expression of a given speaker's attitude entails the non factuality of a representation (2a), but this is not always the case (2b)

(2) a. I am afraid that he does not misses me
b. It's scary that he does not misses me

On the other hand the non-factuality of a representation may be encoded by means other than speaker's attitude markers, such as hypothetical subordinating conjunctions (3a), or alternative constructions (3b):

(3) a. if he misses me, I am happy
b. either he misses me or he doesn't love me

The association of a given attitude marker within a given factuality value is not entirely predictable. Sometimes, even the well-established identification of a certainty attitude with a factual value, which is posited as an axiom, for example in FactBank (Sauri and Pustejovsky, 2012), has to be reconsidered. Let us examine Example 4, where the non factual predicate "I think" and the certainty adverb "surely" impose respectively a non factual and a certainty value to the same event "there will come a time in my veterinary career that I don't get quite so ridiculous when confronted with a puppy"

(4) Sometimes I think that surely, eventually, there will come a time in my veterinary career that I don't get quite so ridiculous when confronted with a puppy.

Many annotation schemes tend to mix these two distinct notions. This is also the case in FactBank.

We claim that both from a theoretical point of view and because of the different purposes that an annotation of factuality and an annotation of speaker's attitude may have (factuality mining and opinion mining respectively) two different levels of annotation and two different annotation schemes should be provided for these two semantic dimensions. While this introduces a certain degree of redundancy, it also enhances clarity, flexibility, and completeness of the annotation, reflecting a theoretically valid distinction.

4 Annotation units

Factuality and speaker's attitude are often encoded by plenty of heterogeneous markers, both within a language and across languages (see also Morante and Sporleder (2012)). We believe that language-specific units of analysis should be determined only *after* cross-linguistic, functional categories have been defined. The lack of a functional background may lead to incomplete annotation schemes, if they are mainly based on the preliminary recognition of a set of markers prototypically connected with modality (such as modal verbs, modal adverbs or modal tags such as 'I guess'/'I believe'). Indeed, the cross-linguistic view of modality shows that there are various encoding strategies that can be overlooked by adopting a purely "lexical" approach.

Concerning factuality, for example, the non factual status of an event is determined not only by its occurence in the scope of a negation or a non factive predicate, but possibly also by an alternative coordinative construction (Mauri (2008)), see (3b) above.

Concerning speaker's attitude, future forms may function as epistemic markers with non-futural temporal reference, as exemplified by the English Future will in (Ex.(5), Nuyts (2006)) and by similar structures in German and in other Romance languages:

(5) Someone's knocking at the door. That will be John.

Similarly, past forms may be used as non-factual (specifically, counterfactual) markers (Fleischman (1995)) not only when they are under the scope of conditional markers (6a) but also when they are used in independent clauses (6b):

(6) a. Se lo sapevo venivo (Colloquial Italian) 'If I knew, I would come'

b. Io ero il principe e tu la principessa (Colloquial Italian) '(Let's pretend) I'm[past] the prince and you're the princess'

Modal particles are another common means for expressing modality. Though easily identifiable in texts, modal particles such as German 'denn' or English 'so' (Ex. 7a and 7b, De Haan (2006)) are somewhat neglected as triggers in the available annotation schemes, and this may be in part due to the difficult classification of their semantic contribution to the textual chunk containing them:

(7) a. Kommt er denn (German) 'Will he really come?'/'Will he come after all?'

b. There is so a Santa Claus!

As for the scope of the modal trigger, we claim that a distinction has to be made between factuality and speaker's attitudes. Factuality is a property of an event: it perfectly makes sense to attribute a factual status to each eventuality, as in Factbank. Speaker's attitude, instead, may apply to more or less extended spans of texts, ranging from a single word (8a) to a sequence of sentences (8b) and even to different dialogic turns (8c).

(8) a. It's a simple and (hopefully) nice cross-platform email chess program.

b. Hopefully he gets another shot and he finds a way to use this failure to motivate him to take the next step, to prove that guys like me completely underestimated him.

c. A: E' stato in banca? (Italian) Did he go to the bank? B: credo (Yes, I) think (so)

Current annotation schemes tend to consider the sentence as the domain within which the effects of a marker signalling the speaker's attitude are visible. Instead, we propose therefore not to aprioristically determine the scope of a trigger but to leave the annotator to identify it.

5 Implementation

The annotation model we are currently developing for both factuality and speaker's attitude is modular, language independent, and data-driven. The specific schemes for the annotation of triggers and markables are described below.

5.1 Schemes

Tables 1 and 2 show the annotation schemes for the elements *markable* and *trigger* respectively. Markables are all of the linguistic objects marked for *factuality* and all those marked for (speaker's) *attitude*. Triggers are those linguistic expressions that determine the factuality and attitude readings of the markables. Working with a functional layer allows us to use the same categories across languages. Markables are selected directly by the annotators and marked with the pre-specified attitude and factuality attributes, while linguistic realisations of triggers are pre-specified in a language-dependent fashion. Cross-language annotations can thus always be compared at the functional level, even in languages which code modality through very different linguistic expressions.

Table 1: Annotation categories for the *markable*

ATTITUDE	no		
	yes	epistemic	committment
			evidential
		deontic	manipulative
			volition
		valutative	axiological
			appreciative
			apprehensional
FACTUALITY	factual		
	non_factual		
	counterfactual		

The modal values in Table 1 are organised in a hierarchical structure, thereby allowing for a more flexible application of the annotation. If the annotator is uncertain about, say, the manipulative or volitional value of a markable (it could be the case for certain optatives, for instance), he can simply tag it as a deontic. If he cannot decide about the deontic or epistemic nature of a markable (which is often the case with possibilities), he can simply tag the mark-

Table 2: Annotation categories for the *trigger*, with examples of linguistic expressions which can be used in Romance (e.g. epistemic future) and Germanic languages (e.g. modal particles).

<table>
<tr><td>MORPHOLOGICAL</td><td colspan="2">epistemic future
reportive conditional
other marker</td></tr>
<tr><td rowspan="4">LEXICAL</td><td>verb</td><td>modal verb (which one)
event selecting predicate (ESPs)</td></tr>
<tr><td colspan="2">noun</td></tr>
<tr><td colspan="2">adjective</td></tr>
<tr><td>pragmatic_marker</td><td>adverbial
parenthetical
modal_particle
connective
question_tag</td></tr>
<tr><td>SYNTACTICAL</td><td colspan="2">hypothetical
alternative
deontic</td></tr>
<tr><td colspan="3">OTHER</td></tr>
</table>

able as a modalized linguistic object. We are confident that more fine-grained and coherent annotation can be driven from the annotation of real data, which should be regarded as an incremental dynamic task.

The left-hand column of Table 2 specifies categories that hold cross-linguistically. The linguistic realisations of triggers in the right-hand column are just examples which hold for some languages but would not (necessarily) be the same when considering other languages. Indeed, the annotation of triggers allows for both a general annotation of the syntactic nature of the trigger used (whether it is morphological, lexical or constructional in nature) and for a more language-specific annotation of the specific trigger used in a given language. Working this way has at least two advantages. First, we can compare different means of expressing same modality across languages. Second, we open the possibility of finding *prototypical*, or unmarked, linguistic expressions which serve as triggers for given modalities, much in the spirit of Croft (1991, 2000). Moreover, we think that such an approach may lead to interesting results for the automatic translation of modality.

5.2 Procedure and example

In the first stages of our annotation, we adopted the following procedure:

1. Identification of markables. We worked under the following assumptions:
   - these objects can vary for semantic nature and syntactic extension;
   - the linguistic objects marked for modality and those marked for factuality do not need coincide
2. Identification of triggers.
3. For each markable we specify:
   - its factuality value
   - its attitude value
   - the factuality trigger
   - the attitude trigger
4. For each trigger we specify:
   - its syntactic nature: a morphological element, a lexical element or a syntactic construction
   - the language-specific category used as a marker (for example the epistemic future for Romance languages, the mirative affix in Turkish, etc.)

As for the scope of markables, it should be clear that markables are often nested within each other: by avoiding a predetermination of the extension and the nature of the markables, we can provide an annotation for each relevant element of our corpus, ranging from the entire text, to an embedded single word. Each markable is linked to its own trigger, regardless of the level of embedding of the trigger itself. Technically, this is done via layers of standoff annotation for factuality and attitude, which point to markables and triggers via their id value.

We use Example 9, from the Europarl corpus (Koehn, 2005), to illustrate our annotation procedure and schemes:

(9) In this respect, we should heed the words of von Eieck, and doubtless also those of the great Italian liberal Bruno Leoni, who warned precisely against the risks of an abnormal increase in anti-competition policies.

In Example 9 we can identify six markables:

(m1) we should heed [the words of von Eieck and doubtless also those of the great Italian liberal Bruno Leoni]

(m2) and doubtless also those of the great Italian liberal Bruno Leoni

(m3) who warned precisely against the risks of [an abnormal increase in anti-competition policies]

(m4) the risks of [an abnormal increase in anti competition policies]

(m5) an abnormal increase [in anti-competition policies]

(m6) increase [in anti-competition policies]

They are marked up in text and then annotated for factuality and attitude according to the schemes described above in a standoff manner. For the sake of presentation, we show the annotation of markables and triggers separately in Figure 1, and the standoff annotation of attitude and factuality in Figure 2.

6 Conclusion and outlook

In our model we provide two independent annotation schemes for factuality and speaker's attitude, thus allowing for higher modularity and flexibility.

One of the main features of our model is the treatment of language specific markers of attitude and factuality as attributes of the modality type (which is instead language independent) assigned to each markable. This representation allows us on the one hand to separate the functional and the formal information, and on the other hand to specify how these are related to each other. This makes the proposed annotation scheme a powerful tool for investigating linguistic diversity in the field of modality on the basis of real language data, being thus also useful from the perspective of machine translation systems.

By avoiding a predetermination of the extension of markables and triggers, we can both provide an annotation for each relevant element of our corpus and account for the complex geometry of markables and triggers, which are often nested within each other. We believe that such an approach should improve the calculus of the percolation of modality along dependency trees and discourse relation structures.

The annotation schemes are being tested through manual annotation performed by expert annotators using existing tools such as GATE (Cunningham et al., 2011), MMAX (Müller and Strube, 2006), and BRAT (Stenetorp et al., 2012). Through annotation exercises and customisation we are currently exploring which might best suit our purposes. Intermediate evaluation of inter-annotator agreement is useful to identify inconsistencies in the scheme, and only after this first phase, the annotation will proceed on a larger scale. We are also considering existing collaborative platforms to perform distributed annotation over the web, so as to optimise the contribution of native speakers.

Content-wise, we plan to enrich our model in at least two ways: (1) by providing a coherent model for the annotation of the strength of modality values (certain, probable, impossible; necessary, prohibited, impossible, etc.); (2) by specifying for each modal attitude, the source of the attitude. Interannotator agreement will also be calculated to assess the validity of the scheme.

Concerning data, we are currently using the Europarl's parallel corpus (Koehn (2005)), but we also aim at including other comparable corpora to maximise linguistic diversity (languages outside Europe will be included) and register variation (mainly through the inclusion of spoken corpora).

```
In this respect , <markable id="m1">we should heed the words of von
Eieck, <markable id="m2">and doubtless also those of the great Italian
liberal Bruno Leoni</markable></markable> , <markable id="m3">who
warned precisely against <markable id="m4">the risks of <markable
id="m5">an abnormal <markable id="m6">increase in anti-competition
policies </markable></markable></markable></markable> .
```

```
In this respect , we <trigger id="t1" type="lexical" subtype="verb"
expr="modal_verb"> should</trigger> heed the words of von Eieck, and
<trigger id="t2" type="lexical" subtype="pragmatic_marker" expr="adverb">
doubtless</trigger> also those of the great Italian liberal Bruno
Leoni , <trigger id="t3" type="syntactical" subtype="relative_clause"
expr="who+V">who <trigger id="t4" type="lexical" subtype="verb"
expr="event_selecting_predicate">warned</trigger> precisely against the
<trigger id="t5" type="lexical" subtype="noun">risks</trigger></trigger>
of an <trigger id="t6" type="lexical" subtype="adjective">abnormal
</trigger> increase in anti-competition policies .
```

Figure 1: Markable and trigger annotation of Example 9.

```
<annotation name="factuality">
<factuality ref="m1" value="nonfactual" trigger="t1"/>
<factuality ref="m3" value="factual" trigger="t3"/>
<factuality ref="m4" value="factual" trigger="t4"/>
<factuality ref="m5" value="nonfactual" trigger="t5"/>
</annotation>

<annotation name="attitude">
<attitude ref="m1" value="deontic" type="manipulative" trigger="t1"/>
<attitude ref="m2" value="epistemic" type="commitment" trigger="t2"/>
<attitude ref="m4" value="deontic" type="manipulative" trigger="t4"/>
<attitude ref="m6" value="valutative" type="apprehensional" trigger="t6"/>
</annotation>
```

Figure 2: Factuality and Attitude annotation for markables of Example 9. Values for pointers are those shown in the annotation in Figure 1.

References

Baker, K. et al. (2010). SIMT SCALE 2009 - Modality Annotation Guidelines, Technical Report. Johns Hopkins, Baltimore.

Baker, K., B. Dorr, M. Bloodgood, C. Callison-Burch, N. Filardo, C. Piatko, L. Levin, and S. Miller (2012). Use of modality and negation in semantically-informed syntactic MT. *Computational Linguistics 38*.

Croft, W. (1991). *Syntactic Categories and Grammatical Relations: The Cognitive Organization of Information*. University of Chicago Press.

Croft, W. (2000). Parts of speech as language universals and as language particular categories. In P. Vogel and B. B. Comrie (Eds.), *Approaches to the Typology of Word Classes*, pp. 65–102. Berlin/New York: Mouton de Gruyter.

H. Cunningham et al. 2011. *Text Processing with GATE (Version 6)*.

De Haan, F. (2006). Typological approaches to modality. In W. Frawley (Ed.), *The expression of modality*, pp. 27–69. Mouton de Gruyter.

Fleischman, S. (1995). Imperfective and irrealis. In J. L. Bybee and S. Fleischman (Eds.), *Modality in discourse and grammar*, pp. 519–551. John Benjamins.

Hendrickx, I., A. Mendes, and S. Mencarelli (2012). Modality in text: a proposal for corpus annotation. In *Proc. of LREC'12*.

Koehn, P. (2005). Europarl: A Parallel Corpus for Statistical Machine Translation. In *Conference Proceedings: the tenth Machine Translation Summit*, Phuket, Thailand, pp. 79–86. AAMT.

Masini F. and Pietrandrea P. (2010). Magari. *Cognitive Linguistics 21*(1).

Mauri, C. (2008). The irreality of alternatives. *Studies in Language*.

McShane, M., S. Nirenburg, and R. Zacharski (2004). Mood and modality: out of theory and into the fray. *Nat. Lang. Eng. 10*(1), 57–89.

Morante, R. and C. Sporleder (2012). Modality and negation: An introduction to the special issue. *Computational Linguistics 38*(2).

Christoph Müller and Michael Strube. 2006. Multi-level annotation of linguistic data with MMAX2. In S. Braun, K. Kohn, and J. Mukherjee, eds, *Corpus Technology and Language Pedagogy: New Resources, New Tools, New Methods*, pages 197–214. Peter Lang, Frankfurt a.M., Germany.

Nirenburg, S. and M. McShane (2008). Annotating modality. Tech. report, University of Maryland.

Nuyts, J. (2006). Modality: Overview and linguistic issues. In W. Frawley (Ed.), *The expression of modality*, pp. 1–26. Mouton de Gruyter.

Sauri, R. and J. Pustejovsky (2009). Factbank: a corpus annotated with event factuality. *Language Resources and Evaluation 43*(3), 227–268.

Roser Sauri and James Pustejovsky. 2012. Are you sure that this happened? Assessing the factuality degree of events in text. *Computational Linguistics*, 38(2):261–299.

P. Stenetorp, S. Pyysalo, G. Topić, T. Ohta, S. Ananiadou, and J. Tsujii. 2012. BRAT: a web-based tool for NLP-assisted text annotation. In *Proceedings of the Demonstrations at EACL'12*, 102–107, Avignon, France.

Szarvas, G., V. Vincze, R. Farkas, and J. Csirik (2008). The bioscope corpus: annotation for negation, uncertainty and their scope in biomedical texts. In *Proc of BioNLP '08*, Stroudsburg, PA, USA, pp. 38–45.

Vincze, V., G. Szarvas, G. Móra, T. Ohta, and R. Farkas (2010). Linguistic scope-based and biological event-based speculation and negation annotations in the genia event and bioscope corpora. In N. Collier et al. (Eds.), *Proc of the Fourth Int. Symp. for Semantic Mining in Biomedicine*, Cambridge, UK.

Wiebe, J., T. Wilson, and C. Cardie (2005). Annotating expressions of opinions and emotions in language. *Language Resources and Evaluation 39*, 165–210.

Multi-layered Annotation of Non-textual Data for Spatial Information

Kiyong Lee
Korea University, Department of Linguistics
Seoul, Korea
ikiyong@gmail.com

Abstract

Spatial and spatio-temporal information is often carried by non-textual data such as maps, diagrams, tables, or pictures, both still and moving, either embedded in a text or standalone. The annotation of nontextual data raises the following questions: (i) what are the markables and how should they be coded? (ii) how should relevant information be inferred which is implicit in the data? We answer these questions with a multilayered approach.

1 Introduction

Non-textual data such as maps, figures, or pictures, either still or moving, are powerful media that carry spatial or spatio-temporal information. This paper concerns the annotation of such data, whether they are embedded in a text or presented alone. As its basic annotation scheme, it follows *ISO-Space*, a semantic annotation scheme which was proposed by Pustejvosky et al. (2012) for the annotation of spatial information in natural language. It is claimed that *ISO-Space* can be adequately applied to the annotation of non-textual data as well as text data in natural language.

Section 2 presents partial specification of *ISO-Space*, section 3 discusses making references to markables, section 4 deals with understanding conventions, section 5 illustrates multi-layered annotation, and section 6 makes concluding remarks.

2 Partial Specification of *ISO-Space*

Given a text (fragment) t_L of a language L, the annotation scheme $\mathcal{AS}_{isoSpace}$ of *ISO-Space* can be defined formally as a quadruple $<M, E, R, @>$, where M is a nonempty finite set of (some selected) segments of t_L, called *markables*, E a nonempty finite set of elements, called *basic entities*, which are either atomic or composite, R an n-ary (basically binary) relation over E, and $@$ a set of functions from a set of attributes to a set of values for each element e in E and each relation r in R. One particular attribute is an attribute, named `@target`, that anchors a basic atomic entity e in E to a markable m in M. For the general formulation of an annotation scheme $\mathcal{AS}$, we basically follow Lee (2012), which is slightly different from that of Bunt (2010) or Bunt (2011).

The set M of markables consists of all the expressions, i.e., sequences of tokens or words in t_L, that refer to all of the basic entities of each of the types defined by E. These entities include (1) spatial entities, tagged as `PLACE` and `PATH` or (2) entities that are not genuinely spatial, but involve spatial entities, tagged as `EVENT`, `MOTION`, `SPATIAL_NE (named entity)` or `SPATIAL_SIGNAL`. The set R of n-ary links over E include (1) qualitative spatial link, (2) orientation link, (3) movement link, and (4) metric link tagged as `QSLINK`, `OLINK`, `MOVELINK`, and `MLINK`, respectively.

The specification of sets of attribute-value pairs for each of the basic entity types and the links requires a complex listing. Each basic entity e in E and each link r in R has a unique ID, specified with the attribute `@xml:id` in XML representation. Each basic entity e is anchored to a markable in M, specified with the attribute `@target` in standoff annotation and assigned a sequence of tokens as value if t_L is a *tokenized* text. Note that there are two types of basic entities, *atomic* and *composite*. Atomic basic entities are simply anchored to a markable in M, whereas composite basic entities are anchored to other basic entities as well as to markables. The entity type PLACE, for instance, is an *atomic* entity type, while the entity type PATH is a *composite* entity type, for the latter is anchored to PLACEs.

Instead of presenting $\mathcal{AS}_{isoSpace}$ as a whole as is formally defined, we may introduce it only partially and also in an informal way with some illustrations. For this, consider the following text:

(1) Mia drove to Jeju International Airport yesterday.

This sentence contains 8 tokens including a punctuation mark. Out of them, *ISO-Space* selects 6 tokens and treats them as four markables, "Mia", "drove", "to", and "Jeju International Airport", as shown below:

(2) Mia_{token1} drove_{token2} to_{token3} Jeju_{token4} $\text{International}_{token5}$ Airport_{token6} yesterday.

Corresponding to the four markables, four basic entities are introduced: SPATIAL_NE, MOTION, SPATIAL_SIGNAL and PLACE. A link is also introduced: <MOVELINK>. Each of them is specified with a list of appropriate attribute-value assignments with some modifications on the current list of *ISO-Space*, as is represented in XML as follows:[1]

(3)
```
<isoSpace>
<SPATIAL_NE xml:id="sne1"
target="#token1" type="PERSON"
form="NAME"/>
<MOTION xml:id="m1"
target="#token2"
motion_type="MANNER"
motion_class="MOVE_EXTERNAL"/>
<SPATIAL_SIGNAL xml:id="s1"
target="#token3"/>
<PLACE xml:id="pl1"
target="#(token4,token6)"
type="FAC" subtype="AIRPORT"
form="NAME"/>
<MOVELINK xml:id="mvl1"
trigger="#m1" goal="#pl1"
mover="#sne1" goal_reached="YES"/>
</isoSpace>
```

This annotation is then understood as conveying the information that there are four types of basic entities involving spatial information: *spatial named entity, motion, spatial signal*, and *place*, and that there is a relation of linking among these entities. Each entity is further specified with information provided by the assignment of a value to each relevant attribute. The place "Jeju International Airport" is, for instance, specified as FAC (facility type) being an airport. With the attribute @target specified as above, each of the four basic entity types <PLACE>, <MOTION>, <SPATIAL_SIGNAL>, and <SPATIAL_NE> refers to some markable (sequence of tokens) in the text.

The annotation given above then introduces one link, namely <MOVELINK>, among those four basic entities. This link is triggered by the motion (m1) of driving to its goal, the airport (pl1) named "Jeju International Airport", with its agent (driver) being a person (sne1) named "Mia". The link, as is annotated here, thus fully represents the information conveyed by the sentence given above. The annotation as a whole can be formally interpreted in first-order logic, as below:

(4) $\exists\{x, y, e\}[person(x) \wedge named(x, Mia) \wedge airport(y) \wedge named(y, JejuInt.Airport) \wedge move\_external(e) \wedge agent(x, e) \wedge goal(y, e) \wedge reach(x, y)]$

3 Making References to Markables

In annotating a text, each basic entity type can easily refer to a part of it as its markable because texts are considered to be sequences of character strings and can thus be tokenized. On the other hand, if input data are other than a text, then making reference to markables requires more complex processes than the simple process of segmenting a text into character offsets or tokens. In this section, we will show how making references to so-called markables in the

[1] We have introduced attribute-value pairs such as type="PERSON" for the annotion of "Mia", and also type="FAC" and subtype="AIRPORT" for that of "Jeju International Airport".

Figure 1: Deep Breathing ©Ghang Lee

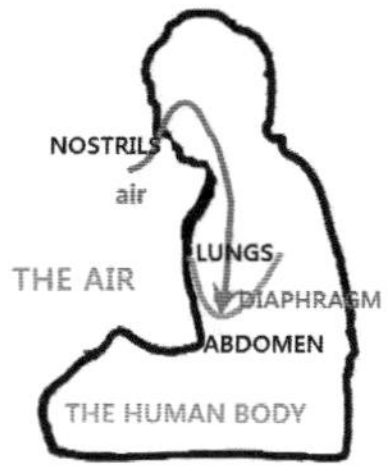

Figure 2: Deep Breathing Annotated ©Ghang Lee

annotation of non-textual data requires techniques more than simply segmenting a text.

Consider Figure 1: *Deep Breathing*. This figure is introduced as part of a guidebook for teaching how to breathe deep down to the abdomen by expanding the diaphragm during the Zen meditation. This figure cannot be segmented into character offsets or tokens, for it contains no characters at all. It rather consists of several geometric objects: (1) an area totally enclosed with a boundary line and an open area outside of it, (2) a curved line located within the enclosed area, and (3) a directed line, namely, arrow entering the upper part of the enclosed area and then reaching that curved line located at the lower part of the enclosed area.

The description of these objects may have to be more explicit for the purposes of computing, perhaps requiring the use of such notions as pixels, coordinates, orientations or topological properties to make them referable as markables. From ordinary linguistic points of view, however, such a specification seems to go beyond the level of semantic representation. It is too complicated to focus on relevant information from the given figure. Instead, we can propose a conventionally more acceptable linguistic technique. Namely, it is to assign a unique name to each of these geometric objects, thus making them uniquely identifiable within a restricted domain and producing a figure such as Figure 2: *Deep Breathing Annotated*. Such a naming technique is especially plausible because the original figure is accompanied by a title that tells what is being depicted. Because of its title *Deep Breathing*, we can conjecture that the figure depicts the process of deep breathing, sometimes called *diaphragmatic breathing*, that undergoes the expansion of the diaphragm or the abdomen.

With such knowledge, we can give names to (1) the two spatial areas: the enclosed area is named THE HUMAN BODY, that represents the shape of the human body with a sitting posture, whereas the open area outside it is named THE AIR; (2) the three relevant points: the first point is named NOSTRILS, which lies on the upper left boundary of the enclosed area, the second point, named LUNGS, which is located at the left middle part of the enclosed area, and the third point, named ABDOMEN, which is located at the mid-lower part of the same enclosed area; and (3) the two lines: the arrow is named IN_PATH, which starts from THE AIR area, goes through the NOSTRILS and the LUNGS and terminates at the ABDOMEN, whereas the other line is named DIAPHRAGM, which is shown to be stretched to the ABDOMEN. We should also be able to recognize two motions: one motion is that of an object named `air` which follows through IN_PATH, and the other motion is that of the DIAPHRAGM that expands from the LUNGS down to the ABDOMEN. Here, two moving objects, `air` and DIAPHRAGM can be treated of type SPATIAL_NE, named entities involving motions in space.

With all these names specified as above, *ISO-Space* can now be applied to the annotation of the whole figure, as represented in XLM below . Besides introducing two spatial named entities (sne1) and (sne2), it annotates two big areas, one enclosed (pl1) and the other open (pl2), the four places or points (pl3, pll4, pl5, pl6) in the enclosed area as parts of the HUMAN BODY, and a path (pl) from the open area (pl2), named THE AIR, to the ABDOMEN (pl6) involving a MOVE_IN motion of air (sne1). There are also two types of links: (1) five `QSLINK`s that relate each of the four places as well as the path to the HUMAN BODY (pl1) and (2) two MOVELINKs, one of which (mvl1) annotates the process of breathing air down to the ABDOMEN (pl6), while the other (mvl2) annotates the streching of the DIAPHRAGM (pl5) to the ABDOMEN (pl6).

(5)
```
<isoSpace xml:id="a2">
<SPATIAL_NE xml:id="sne1"
target="#figure2:air"
type="NATURAL" subtype="AIR"/>
<SPATIAL_NE xml:id="sne2"
target="#figure2:DIAPHRAGM"
type="NATURAL"/>
<PLACE xml:id="pl1"
target="#figure2:HUMAN BODY"/>
<PLACE xml:id="pl2"
target="#figure2:THE AIR area"/>
<PLACE xml:id="pl3"
target="#figure2:NOSTRILS"/>
<PLACE xml:id="pl4"
target="#figure2:LUNGS"/>
<PLACE xml:id="pl5"
target="#figure2:DIAPHRAGM"/>
<PLACE xml:id="pl6"
target="#figure2:ABDOMEN"/>
<PATH xml:id="p1"
target="#figure2:ARROW
figure" beginPoint="#pl2"
midPoint="#pl3,#pl4"
endPoint="#pl5"/>
<MOTION xml:id="m1"
motion_type="PATH"
motion_class="MOVE_INTERNALLY"/>
<MOTION xml:id="m2"
motion_type="MANNER"
motion_class="MOVE"/>
<QSLINK xml:id="qsl2"
figure="#pl2" ground="#pl1"
relType="EC(Externally
connected)"/>
<QSLINK xml:id="qsl1"
figure="#pl3" ground="#pl1"
relType="TTP(tangential proper
part)"/>
<QSLINK xml:id="qsl2"
figure="#pl4" ground="#pl1"
relType="NTTP(non-tangential
proper part)/IN"/>
<QSLINK xml:id="qsl2"
figure="#pl5" ground="#pl1"
relType="NTTP(non-tangential
proper part)/IN"/>
<QSLINK xml:id="qsl2"
figure="#pl6" ground="#pl1"
relType="NTTP(non-tangential
proper part)/IN"/>
<MOVELINK xml:id="mvl1"
trigger="#m1" source="#pl2"
goal="#pl6" mover="#sne1"
pathID="#p1" goal_reached="YES"/>
<MOVELINK xml:id="mvl2"
trigger="#m2" source="#pl5"
goal="#pl6" mover="#sne2"
goal_reached="YES"/>
</isoSpace>
```

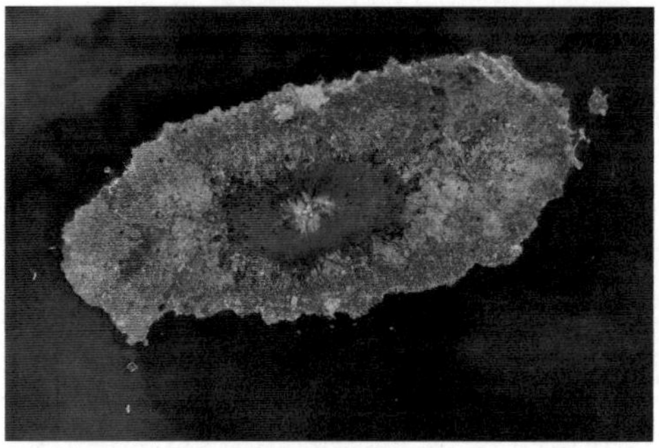

Figure 3: Jeju Island

As is discussed in Mani and Pustejovsky (2012), the relation types such as EC, TTP, and NTTP of qualitative spatial link (QSLINK) are defined by the Region Connection Calculus 8 (RCC-8) (Randell et al., 1992) and (Galton, 2000).[2] This annotation is then understood as stating that air goes into the abdomen in the human body through the nostrils and the lungs by stretching the diaphragm, as claimed by meditation teachers.

Consider another non-textual dataset, Figure 3: *Jeju Island*.[3] This is an aerial photograph of the island. Again from the title of the figure, we understand that the oval shape refers to Jeju Island. With

[2]Here, NTTP may be replaced with IN.

[3]This is a file from the Wikimedia Commons, created by *NASA*. *http://en.wikipedia.org/wiki/File:Cheju_etm_2000097_lrg.jpg*.

Figure 4: Sistine Chapel

plane geometry, we may be able to define the given elliptical region or (near) convex hull and talk about its center or peripheral areas. With some knowledge of reading geographic photographs, we may also be able to derive some geographic information about its mountainous regions, surrounding oceans, attached small isles, and populated areas. We can also refer to each of those areas by drawing (Cartesian) coordinate lines, both horizontal and vertical, as detailed as necessary, over the whole photographed area, thus relying on other than linguistic knowledge or techniques such as word segmentation.[4]

In ordinary conversations, as was just claimed, we may prefer to talk about some areas with their specific names rather than their coordinate values. Naming is an important aspect of the ordinary use of language: for instance, naming places with street number, often framed in mapping coordinates, is found very useful especially when we travel to locate places. Knowing directions is also important. But photographs like Figure 3 do not have any place names or street numbers at all. It also fails to tell which is north or south and which is east or west, although they may allow us to measure a distance from one location to another. In section 5, we discuss multi-layered annotation, showing how such an approach combines various types of information, whether non-linguistic or linguistic, to enrich the annotation of non-textual data such as figures or maps. Note again that one particular layer deals with naming.

Here is a third example, Figure 4: *Sistine Chapel*. It is again an aerial photograph of St. Peter's Basilica in the Vatican with some of its surrounding buildings, one of which is the Sistine Chapel. The photograph itself would not show which building is the Sistine Chapel. The name of the chapel was later printed on the roof of its building in the photograph, Figure 4. We can thus identify the chapel as being located in the upper center of the photograph, standing just next to a smaller dome on the right of the main dome of the basilica when you enter it. Nevertheless, we still do not know how to enter it, except guessing that we might be able to enter it through the basilica. (Yes, you can, if you are a Vatican guard or dignitary.) As is again to be discussed in section 5, this photograph with the name of the destination can provide an important clue for entering the chapel only when it is annotated with other layers of information.

[4] If we are using a Google earth map, then we can simply rely on the geo-coordinate information provided by it.

Table 1: Train Schedule ©Societ Aeroporto Toscano 2002 - 2008

Aeroporto	06:53	09:03	11:03	13:03	15:03	17:03
Pisa Centrale	06:58	09:11	11:11	13:11	15:11	17:11
Pontedera	07:22					
Empoli	07:46					
Firenze SMN	08:22	10:00	12:00	14:00	16:00	18:00
NOTE/REMARKS	A	RV	RV/A	RV	RV/A	RV

A = Except on Sundays and Bank Holidays, **RV** = Fast Regional Connections

4 Understanding Conventions

While presenting information in a visually accessible mode, non-textual data such as maps or figures, or even textual data in a tabular form often fail to provide detailed information unless contextual information supplements them. In this section, we discuss how conventional knowledge helps interpret non-textual data.

Consider Table 1: *Train Schedule*.[5] Schedules for transportations such as trains, buses, ships, and planes are very often presented in a tabular form with columns and rows each identified. To be able to read them, however, one must know some conventions to interpret them. On the first (left-most) column five train stations are listed in order from the Aeroporto station to the Firenze SMN station, the times on each row list the departure or arrival times of trains at each station, and so on. The 09:03 train from Aeroporto stops at Pisa Central, but runs directly to Firenze without stopping at the other two

[5] The departure times for the last two trains are deleted here.

Table 2: Flight Schedule

Ms Mia Lee			
Gimpo-Haneda	(11/30, Fri, 2012)	12:10-14:15	JL0092
Haneda-Gimpo	(12/02, Sun, 2012)	15:30-18:05	JL0093

stations in between. One gets all this information if he or she knows how to read the schedule. If one does not know about the convention of presenting such schedules for transportation, she or he may fail to get necessary information.[6]

Here is another example: a flight schedule given in a tabular form, provided by a travel agent. Knowing some conventions of printing out flight schedules, we get proper information about (1) the customer Ms Mia Lee, who was traveling from Gimpo Airport to Haneda Airport and then from Haneda back to Gimpo, (2) the respective departure and arrival dates and times of the on-going and return flights, and (3) the names of the carriers.

With such knowledge, we can annotate this table with *ISO-Space*, as shown below.

(6)
```
<isoSpace xml:id="a3">
<SPATIAL_NE xml:id="sne1"
target="#table2:col1,row1:
[token1,token3]" form="NAME"
type="PERSON"/>
<SPATIAL_NE xml:id="sne2"
target="#table2:col4,row2:token1"
form="NAME" type="PLANE"
subtype/flightNo="JL0092"/>
<PLACE xml:id="pl1"
target="#table2:col1,row2:token1"
from="NAME" type="FAC"
subtype="AIRPORT" city="SEOUL"
country="KR"/>
<PLACE xml:id="pl2"
target="#table2:col1,row2:token3"
from="NAME" type="FAC"
subtype="AIRPORT" city="TOKYO"
country="JP"/>
<PATH xml:id="p1"
begingPoint="#pl1"
endPoint="#pl2"/>
<MOTION xml:id="m1"
motion_type="MANNER"
motion_class="LEAVE"/>
<MOTION xml:id="m2"
motion_type="MANNER"
motion_class="REACH"/>
<MOTION xml:id="m3"
motion_type="MANNER"
motion_class="MOVE_EXTERNAL"/>
<MOVELINK xml:id="mvl1"
trigger="#m1,#m2" mover="#sne1"
means="#sne2" source="#pl1"
goal="#pl2" goal_reached="YES"
pathID="#p1"/>
</isoSpace>
```

Here three <MOTION> elements are not anchored at all, but only understood through some conventional knowledge involving air flights. These elements should be introduced in order to be able to annotate the departure and arrival-related spatio-temporal information provided in the second and third rows of table 2.

As can be noted very easily, *ISO-Space* deals with spatial information only. To annotate temporal information, it should be applied jointly with *ISO-TimeML* (2012). We can then make the example more interesting and sensible, by annotating various quantitative information of spatio-temporal measurements such as time amount, durations, frequency, distance, and also the tense and modal property of motions or events in general. Lee (2012) has already argued that such a joint application is possible because both *ISO-Space* and *ISO-TimeML* are designed to be interoperable.

5 Multi-layered Annotation

As is argued by Berg et al. (2010) and is well proven by Google Earth map resources, no single map can provide all of the necessary geographic information, thus requiring several layers of a map. If a single map is marked up with all the information, it cannot be parsed. On the other hand, if it is just an aerial photograph, it may not contain enough information, for instance, to tell which town is which and which road is which. This could be the case with linguistic annotation, too. If a single text is tokenized and annotated with all sorts of grammatical or seman-

[6]Strcitly speaking, these tables are only partially *non-textual*. They are non-textual in the sense that they are laid out differently from the ordinary text data.

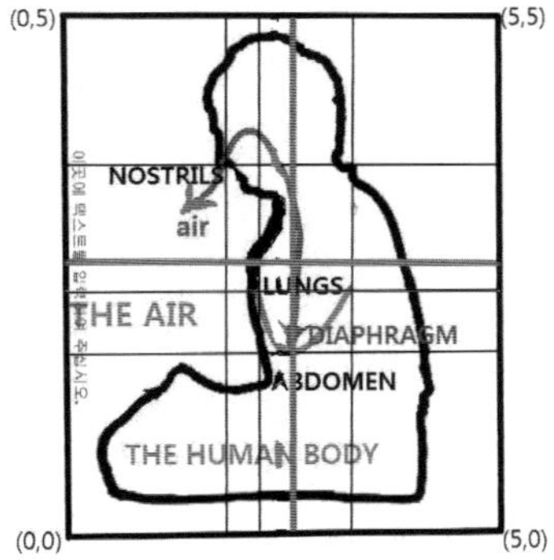

Figure 5: Deep Breathing Figure Segmented ©Ghang Lee

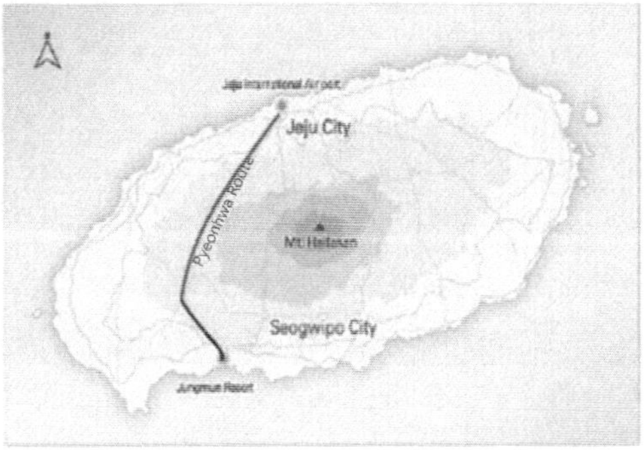

Figure 6: Jeju Island-annotated

tic information, all the information may be too tangled up to be retrieved. LAF (2012) thus requires standoff annotation, as opposed to in-line annotation, while allowing multi-layered annotation of linguistic information. Accordingly, we also argue that a multi-layered approach is not only suitable, but required for the annotation of non-textual data as well as textual data.

For illustration, consider again the figures of deep breathing. In section 3, we have discussed two figures, Figure 1:*Deep Breathing* and Figure 2:*Deep Breathing Annotated*. We have then argued how *ISO-Space* can be adequately applied to annotate the figure of deep breathing by making references to the entity names specified in the second figure. Nevertheless, one may argue that naming alone is not fine-grained enough to identify regions and other spatial entities for some technical applications such as drawing cartoons or architectural designs or even annotating them. In addition to the technique of naming, we thus propose another technique as providing an additional layer of making it possible to refer to markables in both textual and non-textual data.

This technique is a well-known technique of segmenting data, whether textual or not, into smaller constituents. Just like maps with geo-coordinates, each (two-dimensional) figure in a text is to be treated like a Cartesian plane, divided into small areas with their coordinates specified.[7] Then the character strings and some defining points of the region or its parts such as the nostrils, the lungs, the diaphragm, and the abdomen should be identified strictly in terms of those coordinates, just as a text is segmented into tokens based on character offsets.

This technique can be illustrated with the figure of deep breathing. In addition to those two figures, introduced in 3, we can introduce one more figure, Figure 5: *Deep Breathing Figure Segmented*. This third figure treats the whole region as a two-dimensional Cartesian plane, segmented into 5 x 5 areas with unequal sizes.[8] Horizontal and vertical lines are drawn in such a way that some relevant points can be identified with some of their intersections. The position of the nostrils, for instance, is identified with the point (1,4). The non-stretched diaphragm can also be identified as a line segment from (2,2) to (4,2), while its mid-point is being stretched to the point (3,1). Likewise, all of the relevant areas can also be identified by drawing additional lines, if necessary, that segment the whole area into much smaller areas. This then requires another layer of representing the whole figure.

For another illustration, consider the following map of Jeju Island, Figure 6: *Jeju Island-annotated*.[9] Unlike the aerial photograph of Jeju, Figure 3, this new figure has names for several locations: (1) Mt. Halla for the mountain located in the center of the island, (2) Jeju City, Seogwipo, and Jungmun Resort for three populated areas, and Jeju International

[7]Geo-coordinates or other map reading coordinates are particular instances of the Cartesian coordinate.

[8]Quantative information is irrelevant for this particular example.

[9]This file is copyrighted by Jeju Special Self-Governing Province. ©Jejumaster@juju.go.kr. The red line, indicating the Pyeonghwa Route, is added by the author.

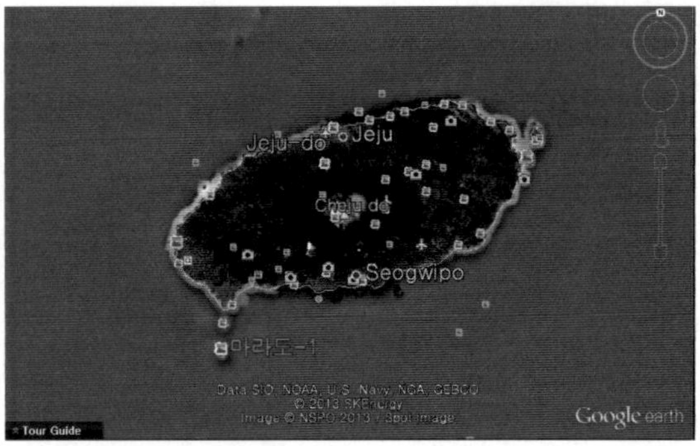

Figure 7: Jeju Google Earth

Airport for the airport, and Pyeonghwa Route for a highway mostly connecting the airport and Jungmun Resort. The two figures offer different types of geographic information: Figure 3 shows the elevation of each part of the island, while Figure 6 provides information more for traveling around the cities on the island. In Figure 6, there is a little arrow on the leftmost upper corner pointing to the north, providing directional information. With this information, we know that the airport is located in the north central boundary of the island. Combined together, these two figures can provide a lot of information that we may or may not be able to derive from a text alone.

Here is a map of the same island, Figure 7 *Jeju Google Earth*[10], with the old romanized name "Cheju do" of the Jeju Province.[11] Besides some place names printed on it, the map contains a lot of tiny buttons, either square-shaped or camera-shaped. As any of the buttons is kept being clicked, it keeps displaying different layers of the map with more detailed information, texts or photos. The Google earth map is thus a typical example of displaying information in layers.

Finally, consider a map for the Sistine Chapel in the Vatican, Figure 8: *How to Get to the Sistine Chapel.*[12] This map guides one from Piazza Pio XII,

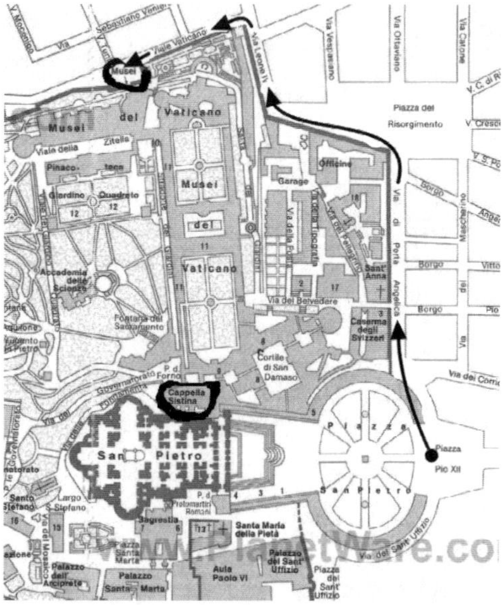

Figure 8: How to Get to the Sistine Chapel

which is just at the entrance to Piazza San Pietro, to the Vatican Museums following the sequence of the arrows going through the roads, named *Via di Porta Angelica*, *Via Leone IV*, and *Viate Vaticano*. There she could enter the museums and all the way to the chapel, named *Capella Sistina* in Italian.

6 Concluding Remarks

This paper applies *ISO-Space* to the annotation of non-textual data such as maps and figures or even some textual data presented in a tabular form because spatial information is very often carried by such data. In annotating such data, one difficulty was how to anchor such basic entities as `PLACE` and `PATH` to parts of the data, since pictures and figures, unlike texts, cannot be tokenized. Another difficulty arose from the understanding of various symbols or conventional cues in visual data. A non-location entity `MOTION` of *ISO-Space*, for instance, is seldom mentioned explicitly, but only expressed implicitly

[10]Created by U.S. Department of State Geographer, ©2013 Google, ©2009 Geo-Basis-DE/BKG, DATA SIO, NOAA, U.S. Navy, NGA, GEBCO.

[11]The place name "Jeju-do" is ambiguous: it may mean either the *island* or the *province* of Jeju. The name "Jeju" itself is also ambiguous: it may refer to either the *city* or the *province* of Jeju.

[12]Except for the paths to the entrance to the Vatican Museums marked by the author, this map is provided by PlanetWare.com with the following note: Use this map on your web site - copy and paste the code below: `<a href="http://www.planetware.com/map/vatican-city-map-scv-vat_ce.htm"> <img src ="http://www.planetware.com/i/map/SCV/vatican-city-map.jpg" width="1200" height="899"/></a><br/> Map from <a href="http://www.planetware.com/">PlanetWare.com</a>.`

with a little pointed arrow, as in Figure 1 or Figure 8. We have argued that such difficulties can be overcome if different layers of visual data are presented and also if various types of information from those data are combined in a consistent way. We have also proposed two conventional techniques for the treatment of markables in annotation: one is to name relevant elements in non-textual data and another is to segment figures in a referable way, for instance, with coordinates. Naming and segmentation are then shown to be providing different layers of annotation, as needs arise.

We have, however, treated these issues simply as technical issues for linguistic purposes only. We have thus avoided discussing any theoretical implications that may go beyond the domain of linguistic annotation, although we have not explicitly demarcated the line between what is linguistic and what is not. A question still remains whether the annotation of non-textual data or multimedia is part of linguistic work. For computing purposes, however, more serious questions may be raised. One could ask how non-human agents can annotate such non-textual data for spatial or spatio-temporal information. Towards answering these questions, more work should be done on multimedia or motion tagging, as discussed in Mani and Pustejovsky (2012), and more serious references should be made to some initiatives that exist in GIS(Geographic Information System)-related communities.

Acknowledgements

I own many thanks to Suk-jin Chang, Jae-Woong Choe, Roland Hausser, Hwan-Mook Lee, Ghang Lee, Chongwon Park, and four anonymous reviewers for their very constructive and detailed comments that helped improve the paper.

References

Berg, Mark de, Otfried Cheong, Marc van Kreveld and Mark Overmars. 2010. *Computational Geometry: Algorithms and Applications*, 3rd edition. Springer, Berlin.

Bunt, Harry. 2010. A methodology for designing semantic annotation languages exploiting syntactic-semantic iso-morphisms. In: A. Fang, N. Ide and J. Webster (eds.) *Proceedings of ICGL 2010, the Second International Conference on Global Interoperability for Language Resources*, pp. 29-45. Hong Kong City University.

Bunt, Harry. 2011. Introducing abstract syntax + semantics in semantic annotation, and its consequences for the annotation of time and events. In E. Lee and A. Yoon (eds.), *Recent Trends in Language and Knowledge Processing*, pp. 157-204. Hankukmunhwasa, Seoul.

Galton, Antony. 2000. *Qualitative Spatial Change*. Oxford University Press, Oxford.

ISO 24612:2012(E) *Language resource management - Linguistic annotation framework (LAF)*, International Organization for Standardizations, Geneva.

ISO 24617-1:2012(E) *Language resource management - Semantic annotation framework - Part 1: Time and events (SemAF-Time, ISO-TimeML)*. International Organization for Standardizations, Geneva.

Lee, Kiyong. 2012. Towards interoperable spatial and temporal annotation schemes. *Proceedings of the Joint ISA-7, SRSL-3, and I2MRT Workshop on Semantic Annotation and the Integration and Interoperability of Multimodal Resources and Tools*, a satellite workshop (26-27 May 2012) held in conjunction with LREC 2012. Istanbul.

Mani, Inderjeet, and James Pustejovsky. 2012. *Interpreting Motion: Grounded Representations for Spatial Language*. Oxford University Press, Oxford.

Pustejovsky, James, Jessica Moszkowics, and Marc Verhagen. 2012. The current status of ISO-Space. *Proceedings of the Seventh Workshop on Interoperable Semantic Annotation (ISA-7)*, a satellite workshop held in conjunction with LREC 2012. Istanbul.

Randell, David A., Zahn Cui, and Anthony G. Cohn. 1992. A spatial logic based on regions and connection. *Proceedings of the Third International Conference on Knowledge Representation and Reasoning*, pp. 165-175. Morgan Kaufman, San Mateo, CA.

Capturing Motion in ISO-SpaceBank

James Pustejovsky
Brandeis University
jamesp@cs.brandeis.edu

Zachary Yocum
Brandeis University
zyocum@brandeis.edu

Abstract

This paper presents the first description of the motion subcorpus of ISO-SpaceBank (MotionBank) and discusses how motion-events are represented in ISO-Space 1.5, a specification language for the representation of spatial information in language. We present data from this subcorpus with examples from the pilot annotation, focusing specifically on the annotation of motion-events and their various participants. These data inform further discussion of outstanding issues concerning semantic annotation, such as quantification and measurement. We address these questions briefly as they impact the design of ISO-Space.

1 Introduction

The goal of ISO-Space is to provide a specification of an annotation language for encoding spatial and spatiotemporal information as expressed in natural language texts. Section 2 enumerates the elements of syntax in ISO-Space 1.5. Section 3 presents data from the MotionBank pilot annoation effort (a subcorpus of ISO-SpaceBank). In the subsequent discussion we focus specifically on relations pertaining to motion, and discuss only limited aspects of topological, orientational, and measurement relations. Section 4 contains discussion of outstanding issues and how they may be tackled.

ISO-Space is being developed as a comprehensive foundation for the annotation of spatial information in natural language text. While there are clearly many issues remaining, we have attempted to follow a strict methodology of specification development, as adopted by ISO TC37/SC4 and outlined in (Bunt, 2010) and (Ide and Romary, 2004), and as implemented with the development of ISO-TimeML (Pustejovsky et al., 2005) and others in the family of SemAF standards.

As reported in (Pustejovsky et al., 2013), ISO-Space is designed to capture both spatial and spatiotemporal information. While still in development, it is clear that the conceptual inventory for spatial language annotation must at least include the following notions:

(1) a. Locations (regions, spatial objects): Geographic and geopolitical places.
b. Entities participating in spatial relations.
c. Paths: routes, lines, turns, arcs.
d. Topological relations: *in, connected.*
e. Direction and Orientation: *North, down.*
f. Time and space measurements: *20 miles away, for two hours.*
g. Object properties: intrinsic orientation, dimensionality.
h. Frames of Reference: absolute, intrinsic, relative.
i. Motion: tracking objects over time.

In the following discussion, we report on the annotation of motion-events and participants, as part of the developing ISO-SpaceBank corpus, and discuss the issues arising with incorporating movement within a spatial representation language.

2 ISO-Space 1.5

In this section, we present a brief description of the ISO-Space 1.5 specification. Note that examples are annotated only with those syntactic elements and attributes which are relevant to the discussion.

2.1 Location Tags

Place Tag The attributes for the PLACE tag are largely inherited from SpatialML (Mani et al., 2010), with some minor additions. This tag is used to annotate geographic entities like lakes and mountains, as well as administrative entities like towns and counties.

(2) a. I camped next to the municipal [**building**$_{pl1}$].
PLACE(id=pl1, form=NOM, dcl=FALSE, countable=TRUE)
b. I traveled north to northern [**Lago Maracaibo**$_{pl2}$].
PLACE(id=pl2, form=NAM, dcl=FALSE, countable=TRUE)

The `form` attribute distinguishes nominal forms (2a) from regions with proper names (2b).

The ISO-Space `mod` attribute is included here because it is substantially different from its counterpart in SpatialML (MITRE, 2007).[1] The ISO-Space `mod` attribute is intended to capture cases like *tall building*, *long trail*, or *the higher observation deck*, where *tall*, *long* and *higher* do not constrain the location of the entity but they do contribute spatial information.

ISO-Space locations tags includes a Document Creation Location or `dcl` attribute. The DCL is a special location that serves as the "narrative location". If a document includes a `dcl`, it is generally specified at the beginning of the text, similarly to the manner in which a Document Creation Time is specified in TimeML (Pustejovsky et al., 2005).

The `countable` attribute is used to distinguish regions referred to with countable sortals (*cities, lakes*) and mass sortals (*highlands, countryside*).

Path Tag The PATH tag is used to capture locations where the focus is on the potential for traversal or functions as a boundary. This includes common nouns as in (3a) and (3b), as well as proper names as in (3c). The attributes of the PATH tag are a subset of the attributes of the PLACE tag, but with the additional `beginID`, `endID`, and `midIDs` attributes. The PATH tag is intended to capture only non-eventive paths, which are treated as inherently non-directional. As such, the `beginID` and `endID` attributes simply indicate bounding points rather than directionality. Table 1 summarizes the attributes for the PATH tag.

Attribute	Value
id	p1, p2, p3, ...
beginID	ID of a location tag
endID	ID of a location tag
midIDs	list of IDs of midpoint locations
form	NAM or NOM
elevation	a MEASURE ID
mod	a spatially relevant modifier
countable	TRUE or FALSE
quant	a generalized quantifier

Table 1: PATH Tag Attributes.

(3) a. ...I arrived at the end of the [**road**$_{p1}$].
b. ...a massive mountain [**range**$_{p2}$] that hugs the west [**coast**$_{p3}$] of Mexico.
c. I followed the [**Pacific Coast Highway**$_{p4}$] along the coastal mountains ...

Non-Consuming Location Tags It is often useful to identify locations that are not mentioned explicitly in the text. In such cases, ISO-Space allows for non-consuming location tags. For example, a non-consuming PLACE tag would be necessary in the case of *John climbed to 9,000 feet* where the elevation *9,000 feet* indirectly references a location that is not associated with any extent in the text.

2.2 Non-Location Tags

While location tags essentially designate a region of space that can be related to other regions on space, ISO-Space allows for non-location elements of a text to be coerced into behaving like a region of space so that they may participate in the same kinds of relationships. There are three of these kinds of non-location tags that may behave like locations in ISO-Space: SPATIAL_E, EVENT and MOTION.[2]

Spatial Entity The SPATIAL_E (spatial entity) tag is intended to capture any entity that is both located in space and participates in an ISO-Space link tag, as illustrated in (4). Attributes include: `id`, `form`, `mod`, `countable`, and `quant`.

(4) [**David**$_{se1}$] passed three [**cars**$_{se2}$] on the road.

[1]Given this discrepancy with SpatialML, it is likely that the ISO-Space annotator will have to perform some "clean-up" of the PLACE elements that are inherited from a SpatialML annotation. This issue will be taken up in the annotation guidelines, though, as it is not relevant to this specification.

[2]Note that, depending on the annotation task, annotating these tags may not be the responsibility of the ISO-Space annotator. Instead, capturing this kind of information may be left to other annotation schemes and it will be left to the ISO-Space annotator to recognize when such an element should participate in an ISO-Space link tag.

Event The EVENT tag captures events that do not involve a change of location but are directly related to another ISO-Space element by way of a link. Events are inherited directly from the ISO-TimeML annotation scheme (Pustejovsky et al., 2005) and require no further specification in ISO-Space.

Spatial Signal The SPATIAL_SIGNAL tag captures relation words or phrases that supply information to an ISO-Space link tag. Signals are typically prepositions or other function words that specify the particular relationship between two ISO-Space elements. Attributes include: id, cluster, and semantic_type.

Adjunct The ADJUNCT tag captures additional *event-path* or *manner-of-motion* information that is not contributed directly by a motion verb, but rather by a satellite word or phrase. PATH motion adjuncts are often prepositions (e.g, *to* and *from*). Adjuncts of type MANNER supply manner of motion information (e.g., *by car*). Notice in (5d) that multiple adjuncts may contribute to a single motion.

(5) a. John walked [**to**$_{a1}$] the store.
b. John left [**for**$_{a2}$] Boston.
c. John traveled [**by car**$_{a3}$].
d. John arrived [**by bike**$_{a4}$] [**at**$_{a5}$] the trailhead.

Measure The MEASURE tag is used to capture distances and dimensions for use in an MLINK or to fill the elevation attribute for a location tag. See (Pustejovsky et al., 2013) for more details.

2.3 Spatial Relation Links

There are four relationship tags in ISO-Space defined as follows:

(6) a. QSLINK – for qualitative spatial relations;
b. OLINK – for orientation relations;
c. MOVELINK – for movement relations;
d. MLINK – for dimensions of a region or the distance between locations.

Qualitative Spatial Link QSLINKs are used in ISO-Space to capture topological relationships between tag elements captured in the annotation. The relType attribute values come from an extension to the RCC8 set of relations that was first used by SpatialML. The possible RCC8+ values include the RCC8 values (Randell et al., 1992), in addition to IN, a disjunction of TPP and NTPP (cf. Table 2).

Relation	Description
DC	Disconnected
EC	External Connection
PO	Partial Overlap
EQ	Equal
TPP	Tangential Proper Part
TPP_i	Inverse of TTP
NTTP	Non-Tangential Proper Part
$NTTP_i$	Inverse of NTTP
IN	Disjunction of TTP and NTTP

Table 2: RCC8+ Relations.

It is worth noting that while the QSLINK tag is used exclusively for capturing topological relationships, which are only possible between two regions, the figure and ground attributes can accept IDs for both PLACEs and PATHs, which are more traditional regions, as well as SPATIAL_ES, EVENTs, and MOTIONs. In the latter cases, it is actually the region of space that is associated with the location of the entity or event that participates in the QSLINK. That is, the entity or event is coerced to a region for the purposes of interpreting this link.

In practice, a QSLINK is triggered by a SPATIAL_SIGNAL with a semantic_type of TOPOLOGICAL or DIR_TOP (cf. (7) below).

(7) [The book$_{se1}$] is [on$_{s1}$] [the table$_{se2}$].
SPATIAL_SIGNAL(id=s1, cluster="on-1", semantic_type= DIR_TOP)
QSLINK(id=qsl1, figure=sne1, ground=sne2, trigger=s1, relType=EC)

Orientation Link Orientation links describe non-topological relationships. A SPATIAL_SIGNAL with a DIRECTIONAL semantic_type triggers such a link. In contrast to qualitative spatial relations, OLINK relations are built around a specific frame of reference type and a reference point. The attributes for OLINK are listed in Table 3.

The referencePt value depends on the frame_type of the link. The ABSOLUTE frame type stipulates that the referencePt is a cardinal direction. For INTRINSIC OLINKs, the referencePt is the same identifier that is given in the ground attribute. For RELATIVE OLINKs, the identifier for the viewer should be provided as to the referencePt. If the viewer is not explicit in the text, the special value "VIEWER" should be used. Examples of this link are illustrated in (8).

(8) a. [**Boston**$_{pl1}$] is [**north of**$_{s1}$] [**New York City**$_{pl2}$].

Attribute	Value
id	ol1, ol2, ol3,...
relType	ABOVE, BELOW, FRONT, NORTH,...
figure	ID of the location/entity/event that is being related to the ground
ground	ID of the location/entity/event that is being related to by the figure
trigger	ID of a SPATIAL_SIGNAL that triggered the link
frame_type	ABSOLUTE, INTRINSIC or RELATIVE
referencePt	ground location/entity/event ID, cardinal direction, or viewer entity ID
projective	TRUE or FALSE

Table 3: OLINK Attributes.

OLINK(id=ol1, figure=pl1, ground=pl2, trigger=s1, relType="NORTH", frame_type=ABSOLUTE, referencePt="NORTH", projective=TRUE)

b. [The dog$_{se1}$] is [in front of$_{s2}$] [the couch$_{se2}$].
OLINK(id=ol2, figure=sne1, ground=sne2, trigger=s2, relType="FRONT", frame_type=INTRINSIC, referencePt=sne2, projective=FALSE)

Measure Link Measurement relationships are captured with the MLINK tag, as first proposed for ISO-TimeML (Pustejovsky et al., 2010). Currently, this tag describes either the relationship between two spatial objects or the dimensions of a single object (cf. Table 4).

Attribute	Value
id	ml1, ml2, ml3,...
figure	ID of the location/entity/event event that is being related to the ground
ground	ID of the location/entity/event that is being related to by the figure
relType	DISTANCE, LENGTH, WIDTH, HEIGHT, or GENERAL_DIMENSION
val	a MEASURE ID or NEAR, FAR, TALLER, SHORTER,
endPoint1	ID of a location/entity/event at one end of a stative path
endPoint2	ID of a location/entity/event at the other end of a stative path

Table 4: MLINK Attributes.

When an MLINK is used to capture an internal dimension of an object as in (9b) or (9c), the ID of that object should appear in the figure attribute. The annotator may either repeat the identifier in the ground attribute or leave the ground unspecified.

(9) a. The new [**tropical depression**$_{se1}$] was about [**430 miles**$_{me1}$] ([**690 kilometers**$_{me2}$]) west of the [**southernmost Cape Verde Island**$_{pl1}$], they said.
MLINK(id=ml1, relType=DISTANCE, figure=sne1, ground=pl1, val=me1)

b. [**The football field**$_{se2}$] is [**100 yards**$_{me2}$] long.
MLINK (id=ml2, relType=LENGTH, figure=sne2, ground=sne2, val=me2)

c. I [**rode**$_{m1}$] [**30 miles**$_{me4}$] yesterday.
MLINK (id=ml6, relType=general_dimen, figure=m1, ground=m1, val=me4)

2.4 Movement

The treatment of movement in ISO-Space draws heavily from the foundations of lexical semantics in (Talmy, 1985) and the motion-event classifications in (Muller, 1998) and (Pustejovsky and Moszkowicz, 2008). There are two ISO-Space tags which capture movement: MOTION and MOVELINK.

Motion Tag The ISO-Space MOTION tag is a species of TimeML event that involves a change of location or spatial configuration. Table 5 lists the attributes of the MOTION tag.

Attribute	Value
id	m1, m2, m3, ...
motion_type	MANNER, PATH, COMPOUND
motion_class	MOVE, MOVE_EXTERNAL, MOVE_INTERNAL, LEAVE, REACH, DETACH, HIT, FOLLOW, DEVIATE, CROSS, STAY
motion_sense	LITERAL, FICTIVE, INTRINSIC_CHANGE

Table 5: MOTION Tag Attributes.

The motion_type attribute refers to the two major strategies for expressing movement in language: *path* and *manner-of-motion* constructions (Talmy, 1985). This is illustrated in (10), where m indicates a manner contributing component, and p indicates a path contributing component. In the first sentence, the motion verb specifies a path whereas in the second the motion verb specifies the manner of motion. The motions in these sentences are actually of the motion_type COMPOUND since they supply both path and manner information.

(10) a. John arrived$_p$ [by foot]$_m$.

b. John hopped$_m$ [out of the room]$_p$.

Motion classes are taken from (Pustejovsky and Moszkowicz, 2008), which in turn are based on those in (Muller, 1998). These classes are associated with a spatial event structure that specifies the spatial relations between the arguments of the motion verb at different phases of the event. Table 6 lists the set of motion classes and their associated motion-event structures.

The `motion_sense` attribute distinguishes between different kinds of interpretations of motion-events. The LITERAL sense covers motion-events where the mover participant's location changes over time. The FICTIVE sense covers cases where the event involves an atemporal, experiential change in an extrinsic property (e.g., elevation or location). The INTRINSIC_CHANGE sense covers motion verbs that describe change in some intrinsic, spatial characteristic (e.g., height, width, length, shape, etc.). The motivation here is to disambiguate language like *the balloon rose above the building* from *the river rose above the levy*, where a LITERAL interpretation—the river's elevation increased—is inappropriate: the location of the eleavtion of the river is supervenient on the change in the volume of the river, therefore signaling an intrinsic change.[3] The `motion_sense` attribute also captures FICTIVE motion interpretations such as, *the mountain rises above the valley*, where there is no temporal interpretation—the mountain's elevation increasing over time—but rather a purely spatial, atemporal interpretaion predicating spatial characteristics of the mountain over some region.

Movelink Tag MOVELINK tags, which are introduced by MOTION tags, capture information about the path or course a particular motion takes. Table 7 lists the attributes of the MOVELINK link.

The event structures for MOVE_EXTERNAL and MOVE_INTERNAL motion-events require a `ground` location relative to which the motion of the `mover` participant occurs. This location is identified with the `ground` attribute introduced in Table 7 and its use is demonstrated in Example (11a).

Another attribute introduced in Table 7 is `adjunctID`. This attribute takes the identifier of an ATTRIBUTE tag that contributes path or manner information about the event-path of the MOVELINK's triggering motion-event. The use of the `adjunctID` attribute is demonstrated in Example (11b)

[3]While this could be an instance of a metonymic sense extension, such as *the kettle boiled* (per a reviewer's suggestion), we believe this is more specific to the entailments associated with an intrinsic change in an object's spatial extent.

Attribute	Value
`id`	`mvl1, mvl2, mvl3, ...`
`trigger`	ID of a MOTION that triggered the link
`source`	ID of a location/entity/event tag at the beginning of the event-path
`goal`	ID of a location/entity/event tag at the end of the event-path
`midPoint`	ID(s) of event-path midpoint location/entity/event tags
`mover`	ID of the locatin/entity/event whose whose location changes
`ground`	ID of a location/entity/event tag that the `mover`'s motion is relative to
`goal_reached`	TRUE, FALSE, UNCERTAIN
`pathID`	ID of a PATH tag that is identical to the event-path of the triggering MOTION
`adjunctID`	IDs of any ADJUNCT tags that contribute path or manner information to the triggering MOTION

Table 7: MOVELINK Tag Attributes.

(11) a. ... [**we**$_{se1}$] [**passed**$_{m1}$] [**glaciers**$_{p1}$] and [**snowfields**$_{pl1}$] ...
SPATIAL_E (`id=sne1, form=`NOM, `countable=`TRUE)
MOTION (`id=m1, motion_type=`PATH, `motion_class=`MOVE_EXTERNAL, `motion_sense=`LITERAL)
MOVELINK (`id=mvl1, trigger=m1, mover=sne1, ground=p1`)
MOVELINK (`id=mvl2, trigger=m1, mover=sne1, ground=pl1`)

b. [**I**$_{se2}$] [**biked**$_{m2}$] [**into**$_{a1}$] a [**town**$_{pl2}$] at 4pm.
SPATIAL_E (`id=sne2, form=`NOM, `countable=`TRUE)
MOTION (`id=m2, motion_type=`COMPOUND, `motion_class=`REACH, `motion_sense=`LITERAL)
MOVELINK (`id=mvl3, trigger=m2, goal=pl2, mover=sne2, goal_reached=yes, adjunctID=a1`)

2.5 Annotation vs. Axioms

It is important to note that ISO-Space's inventory of explicit representations does not capture the whole picture. Some representations are introduced at the level of abstract syntax by specific axiomatic rules. We introduce the assumed premises for motion briefly, and defer details to the final paper.

Mover Participants The first axiom pertaining to motion in ISO-Space is that, for every motion-event,

Value	Requisite Attributes	Event Structure
MOVE	mover	$_{begin}[location\_of(\texttt{mover})] \not\sim {}_{end}[location\_of(\texttt{mover})]$
MOVE_EXTERNAL	mover, ground	$_{begin...end}[\{\text{DC} \wedge \text{EC}\}(\texttt{mover}, \texttt{ground})]$
MOVE_INTERNAL	mover, ground	$_{begin...end}[\text{IN}(\texttt{mover}, \texttt{ground})]$
LEAVE	mover, source	$_{begin}[\text{IN}(\texttt{mover}, \texttt{source})], {}_{end}[\{\text{DC} \wedge \text{EC}\}(\texttt{mover}, \texttt{source})]$
REACH	mover, goal	$_{begin}[\text{DC}(\texttt{mover}, \texttt{goal})], {}_{end}[\text{IN}(\texttt{mover}, \texttt{goal})]$
DETACH	mover, source	$_{begin}[\text{EC}(\texttt{mover}, \texttt{source})], {}_{end}[\text{DC}(\texttt{mover}, \texttt{source})]$
HIT	mover, goal	$_{begin}[\text{DC}(\texttt{mover}, \texttt{goal})], {}_{end}[\text{EC}(\texttt{mover}, \texttt{goal})]$
FOLLOW	mover, pathID	$_{begin...end}[path\_of(\texttt{mover}) \sim \texttt{pathID}]$
DEVIATE	mover, pathID	$_{begin}[path\_of(\texttt{mover}) \sim \texttt{pathID}], {}_{end}[path\_of(\texttt{mover}) \not\sim \texttt{pathID}]$
CROSS	mover, source, midPoints, goal	$_{begin}[\text{IN}(\texttt{mover}, \texttt{source})], {}_{mid}[\text{IN}(\texttt{mover}, \texttt{midPoints})], {}_{end}[\text{IN}(\texttt{mover}, \texttt{goal})]$
STAY	mover, ground	$_{begin...end}[\{\{\text{RCC8+}\},\{\text{OLINK}\}\}(\texttt{mover}, \texttt{ground})]$

Table 6: Motion Class Event Structures

there exists an entity which fulfills the role of mover for that event. The mover is that participant in the motion-event which undergoes a change in its location. That is to say:

(12) $\forall e \exists x[motion\text{-}event(e) \rightarrow mover(x, e)]$

Event Paths The other essential component of ISO-Space that is generated axiomatically is the event-path created by the mover associated with a motion-event. That is to say:

(13) $\forall e \exists p[motion\text{-}event(e) \rightarrow [event\text{-}path(p) \wedge loc(e, p)]]$

Previous versions of the ISO-Space specification included an event-path tag as part of the concrete syntax, distinct from the non-eventive PATH tag. In fact, the `source`, `goal`, `midPoint` and `pathID` attributes of the MOVELINK tag presume an event-path (although these attributes are often underspecified). The primary motivation for the removal of event-paths as their own category in the concrete syntax is that our abstract syntax axiomatically introduces an event-path for each motion-event.[4]

This decision simplifies the annotation task in that annotators need only identify features of the event-path if the language contributes information about the path of traversal. A bare-manner motion verb, as in *David* ***cycles*** *seriously*, for instance, introduces a completely underspecified event-path. Thus, the following annotation in 14 would be sufficient.

(14) [David$_{se1}$] [cycles$_{m1}$] seriously.
SPATIAL_E (id=se1, text="David", form=NAM)
MOTION (id=m1, text="cycles", motion_type=MANNER, motion_class=MOVE, motion_sense=LITERAL)
MOVELINK (id=mvl1, trigger=m1, source=∅, goal=∅, midPoint=∅, mover=se1, ground=∅, goal_reached=∅, pathID=∅, adjunctID=∅)

[4]Discussions from participants at ISA-7 and ISA-8 were instrumental in leading to this modification in the specification.

3 ISO-SpaceBank Subcorpus Data

The data in this section are tabulated from the pilot annotation of MotionBank, a subcorpus of ISO-SpaceBank consisting of 50 entries (20,877 word tokens) from a travel blog whose author cycled across the Americas. Table 8 presents a breakdown of the tag counts for each ISO-Space tag type. Table 9 lists the counts for each class of motion over the same subcorpus by frequency.

Tag Type	Frequency
PLACE	1313
SPATIAL_E	856
MOVELINK	834
MOTION	794
SPATIAL_SIGNAL	558
ADJUNCT	407
PATH	294
EVENT	186
total	**5308**

Table 8: Tag Counts

To best illustrate the annotation of motion and the various participants, we present one detailed example in full. Sentence (15) is spatially quite rich and it is also notable for the figurative language that is employed. The first item of note is the non-consuming place tag that has been created. In this case the MEASURE ID of *over 6,000 feet* fills the `elevation` attribute of the non-consuming place tag. The ID of this PLACE tag is then used later to fill the `goal` location for the MOVELINK triggered by `m3` (*climbs*).

The second thing to note is that the `motion_sense` attributes for all the MOTION

Motion Class	Frequency
MOVE	183
REACH	177
STAY	130
HIT	62
LEAVE	56
FOLLOW	54
CROSS	54
MOVE_INTERNAL	39
MOVE_EXTERNAL	26
DETACH	11
DEVIATE	2
Total	**794**

Table 9: Motion Class Counts

tags are FICTIVE. This is because the *road* is fulfilling the role of mover and the annotator assumed figurative, atemporal interpretations for the *Departing*, *climbs*, and *climb* motion-events.

(15) a. [**Departing**$_{m2}$] [**Copala**$_{pl11}$], the [**road**$_{p1}$] [**climbs**$_{m3}$] [**to**$_{a1}$] [**over 6,000 feet**$_{me5}$] in [**30 miles**$_{me6}$], and then continues to [**climb**$_{m4}$] while [**hugging**$_{s8}$] an impressive cliff-lined [**ridgeline**$_{p2}$] literally called 'the spine of the devil.' [$\varnothing_{pl12}$]
PLACE (id=pl11, text="Copala", form=NAM, dcl=FALSE, num=SING)
PLACE (id=pl12, text=∅, elevation=me5, dcl=FALSE, num=SING)
PATH (id=p1, midIDs={pl11, pl12}, form=NOM)
PATH (id=p2, text="ridgeline", form=NOM, countable=TRUE)
MEASURE (id=me5, text="over 6,000 feet", value="gt 6000", unit="feet")
MEASURE (id=me6, text="30 miles", value="30", unit="feet")
MLINK (id=ml5, figure=m3, GROUND=m3, relType=GENERAL_DIMENSION, val=m6, endPoint1=pl11, endPoint2=pl12)
MOTION (id=m2, text="Departing", motion_type=PATH, class=LEAVE, motion_sense=FICTIVE)
MOVELINK (id=mvl2, trigger=m2, source=pl11, mover=p1, pathID=p1)
MOTION (id=m3, text="climbs", class=MOVE, motion_sense=FICTIVE)
ADJUNCT (id=a1, text="to", type=PATH)
MOVELINK (id=mvl3, trigger=m3, source=pl11, goal=pl12, mover=p1, goal_reached=TRUE, pathID=p1, ajdunctID=a1)
MOTION (id=m4, text="climb", class=MOVE, motion_sense=FICTIVE)
MOVELINK (id=mvl4, trigger=m4, source=pl12, mover=p1, pathID=p1)
SPATIAL_SIGNAL (id=s8, text="hugging", semantic_type=DIR_TOP)
QSLINK (id=qsl8, relType=DC, figure=p1, ground=p2, trigger=s8)

4 Discussion

Several interesting issues arose during the initial motion annotation efforts with ISO-Space. The first concerns how to handle 'simulated' motion-events. Such events are the kind typical in direction-giving language where a direction-giver may specify a path that is intended to be followed without explicitly specifying a mover participant: *Walk 100 meters and turn right after the store.* Initially, this was dealt with by providing an additional motion_sense value, called SIMULATED, in order to distinguish such uses from the FICTIVE, LITERAL, and INTRINSIC_CHANGE motion senses. After further corpus investigation, however, we have determined that this is a *narrative modality* rather than a specific sense distinction exploited for motion verbs. This deserves further modeling and we are currently investigating this topic.

Another issue that arises, although interestingly, not represented in the present corpus, involves the use of *extent verbs* (Gawron, 2009). This use is seen in the following: *Past the brook, the road* ***narrows***. This shares semantic elements with the FICTIVE sense, but introduces additional constraints not accompanying those uses (as in *the road climbs*, etc.). This is also currently under further investigation.

It is worth pointing out that quantification presents itself again as an issue. ISO-Space 1.4 provides countable and quant attributes for location tags, however these features alone remain insufficient for a complete motion-events semantics. Consider (16), for instance. The annotation captures the quantification over *valley* with the PATH tag p1, and the MOVELINK (mvl1) triggered by *passed* (m1) specifies p1 as a midPoint location.

(16) a. ... [**I**$_{se1}$] [**passed**$_{m1}$] through every small, uninhabited [**valley**$_{p1}$] [$\varnothing_{pl1}$] [$\varnothing_{pl2}$][5] ...
SPATIAL_E (id=sne1, text="I", form=NOM)
path (id=p1, text="valley", form=NOM, mod="small", quant="every")

[5]The symbol ∅ is used here to identify non-consuming tags in the text.

MOTION (id=m1, text="passed", motion_type=PATH, motion_class=CROSS, motion_sense=LITERAL)

MOVELINK (id=mvl1, trigger=m1, source=pl1, goal=pl2, midPoint=p1, mover=sne1, goal_reached=TRUE)

For a proper semantic interpretation, it is essential to produce an interpretation for this sentence where m1 falls under the scope of the quantifier *every*. That is, for *every valley*, there exists a *passing* motion-event. A partial translation is as follows, where $through$ is a stand in for the appropriate QSLINK relation value.

(17) $\forall p_1 \exists m_1 [[valley(p_1) \wedge small(p_1) \rightarrow [pass(m_1) \wedge through(m_1, p_1)]]$

In addressing this issue, ISO-Space 1.5 draws from TimeML's treatment of event quantification in (Bunt and Pustejovsky, 2010; Pustejovsky et al., 2010), to handle examples such as *John taught every Tuesday*. ISO-TimeML captures quantificational scoping relations with a $scopes(scoper, scopee)$ relation. We propose to extend the tag attributes in the ISO-Space with a scopes attribute to capture such relations.

Finally, another desideratum that has been made evident by the pilot annotation data is the ability to capture motion when it occurs in nominal form. That is not to say that all motion-event nominals ought to be treated as instances of motion. For example, while *a **vacation** to Mexico* seems to entail travel, *a summer **vacation*** may not. Additionnally, the participants of motion-event nominals are often underspecified. The pilot annotation guidelines did not sufficiently address the possibility of underspecified mover participants, and consequently, the EVENT tag was employed for nominalized motion-events. Examples from MotionBank where this confusion occurred are italicized in the sentences in Example (18).

(18)
a. The last few days of the *trip* were difficult, including an 8,000 feet *climb* into the Andes.
b. According to Ricardo, bicycle *use* has increased 5 times in the city, and now there are probably between 300,000 and 400,000 *trips* made daily in Bogota by bicycle.
c. Passing through more towns and more *climbs* and *descents* on one lane dirt roads, I eventually climbed into the Cordillera Blanca ...
d. I also received a *tour* of the town from three high school students ...
e. I have now arrived in Yurimaguas, a small city in the jungle, thus ending my two weeks of boat *travel* on the world's largest river system.
f. Many people I have stayed with on this *trip* live in small houses, are poor, own no car, and have little healthcare.

5 Conclusion

In this paper we have presented an initial description of the motion subcorpus of the ISO-Space specification for spatiotemporal and spatial markup of natural language text. Through this discussion we hope to vet some of the remaining issues we have encountered with annotating movement phenemona in natural language. Our expectation is to release the completed MotionBank sub-corpus in June 2013 and subsequently the full SpaceBank corpus in January 2014.

Acknowledgements

This research was supported by grants from the NSF (NSF-IIS 1017765) and the NGA (NURI HM1582-08-1-0018). We would like to thank Jessica Moszkowicz, Marc Verhagen, Harry Bunt, and Kiyong Lee for their contributions to this discussion. We would also like to acknowledge the four anonymous reviewers for their helpful comments. All errors and mistakes are, of course, the responsibilities of the authors.

References

Harry Bunt and J. Pustejovsky. 2010. Annotating temporal and event quantification. In *Proceedings of 5th ISA Workshop*.

Harry Bunt. 2010. A methodology for designing semantic annotation languages exploiting syntactic-semantic iso-morphisms. In *Proceedings of ICGL 2010, Second International Conference on Global Interoperability for Language Resources*.

J.M. Gawron. 2009. The lexical semantics of extent verbs. *San Diego State University*.

Nancy Ide and Laurent Romary. 2004. International standard for a linguistic annotation framework. *Natural Language Engineering*, 10(3-4):211–225.

Inderjeet Mani, Christy Doran, Dave Harris, Janet Hitzeman, Rob Quimby, Justin Richer, Ben Wellner, Scott Mardis, and Seamus Clancy. 2010. Spatialml: annotation scheme, resources, and evaluation. *Language Resources and Evaluation*, 44:263–280. 10.1007/s10579-010-9121-0.

MITRE. 2007. Spatialml: Annotation scheme for marking spatial expressions in natural language. http://sourceforge.net/projects/spatialml/.

Philippe Muller. 1998. A qualitative theory of motion based on spatio-temporal primitives. In Anthony G. Cohn, Lenhart Schubert, and Stuart C. Shapiro, editors, *KR'98: Principles of Knowledge Representation and Reasoning*, pages 131–141. Morgan Kaufmann, San Francisco, California.

James Pustejovsky and Jessica L. Moszkowicz. 2008. Integrating motion predicate classes with spatial and temporal annotations. In *Proceedings of COLING 2008*, Manchester, UK.

James Pustejovsky, Robert Knippen, Jessica Littman, and Roser Saurí. 2005. Temporal and event information in natural language text. *Language Resources and Evaluation*, 39:123–164, May.

James Pustejovsky, Kiyong Lee, Harry Bunt, and Laurent Romary. 2010. Iso-timeml: An international standard for semantic annotation. In *LREC*.

James Pustejovsky, Jessica Moszkowicz, and Marc Verhagen. 2013. A linguistically grounded annotation language for spatial information. Special issue of TAL. Forthcoming.

David Randell, Zhan Cui, and Anthony Cohn. 1992. A spatial logic based on regions and connections. In Morgan Kaufmann, editor, *Proceedings of the 3rd Internation Conference on Knowledge Representation and Reasoning*, pages 165–176, San Mateo.

Leonard Talmy. 1985. Lexicalization patterns: semantic structure in lexical forms. In T. Shopen, editor, *Language typology and semantic description Volume 3: Grammatical categories and the lexicon*, pages 36–149. Cambridge University Press.

Interoperable Annotation in the Australian National Corpus

Steve Cassidy
Department of Computing
Macquarie University
Sydney, Australia
steve.cassidy@mq.edu.au

Abstract

The Australian National Corpus (AusNC) provides a technical infrastructure for collecting and publishing language resources representing Australian language use. As part of the project we have ingested a wide range of resource types into the system, bringing together the different meta-data and annotations into a single interoperable database. This paper describes the initial collections in AusNC and the procedures used to parse a variety of data types into a single unified annotation store.

1 Introduction

The Australian National Corpus (AusNC) is a new project to create a wide ranging resource for research on language in Australia. In contrast to other National Corpora, it is not a new, targeted collection of language data. Instead, the AusNC will manage a range of collections of language use in Australia that will be unified by common meta-data, data and annotation standards and formats. This approach allows us to curate existing important collections and incorporate new collections into a larger whole that may prove more useful than the sum of its parts.

In the long term, AusNC aims to illustrate Australian English in all its variety, situational, social, generational, and ethnic; and to document languages other than English used in Australia, including Aboriginal and Torres-Strait Islander languages, AUSLAN, and the community languages of immigrants. The Corpus also aims to serve a wide range of research disciplines from grammatical and lexical studies to sociolinguistic research and language technology. By including audio and video sources the Corpus hopes to be able to serve researchers interested in acoustics and gesture as well as language technology applications that require this kind of data to train and test computational models.

The pilot project that established the AusNC chose a small number of corpora that were felt to characterise the range of corpora in use by Australian researchers. These include a number of important historical collections that have been used to characterise Australian English in the past. The primary focus of the project was to ingest the corpus text and meta-data into a web accessible form and provide a way of browsing this data and publishing meta-data records to the Research Data Australia directory[1]. However, as a part of the ingestion process, we undertook to parse as much annotation data as possible and convert it to an RDF format (Cassidy, 2010) so that it might be used in a future version of the technical infrastructure.

This paper describes some aspects of the process by which meta-data and annotations were extracted from these corpora and the measures we took to ensure the interoperability of the data in the AusNC platform.

2 Overview of Corpora

The corpora included in the initial collection are drawn from a range of disciplines and contain a varied amount of meta-data and annotation. In summary, the corpora are:

[1] http://researchdata.ands.org.au/australian-national-corpus

- **The Australian Corpus of English (ACE)**: Written language, some simple XML like markup for header, bylines etc.

- **The Australian ICE Corpus**: Written and spoken language, XML like markup following the ICE standards.

- **The Corpus of Oz Early English (COOEE)**: Historical texts with minimal markup.

- **The Monash Corpus of Spoken English**: transcribed audio of conversations in Word format, speaker turn annotation

- **The Griffith Corpus of Australian Spoken English**: transcribed audio of conversations in PDF format with embedded Conversation Analysis markup.

- **The AustLit collection**: TEI formatted samples of Australian fiction.

- **The Mitchell and Delbridge Corpus**: audio recordings with time aligned word and phonetic annotations.

- **The Braided Channels Research Collection**: video recordings with transcriptions in Word format, speaker turn annotations, roughly time aligned with video.

All of these corpora are hand-annotated - the annotation was done as part of the data collection and served the research in a particular discipline. There is clearly scope for adding more machine-generated annotation such as sentence segmentation and POS tagging, but doing so was beyond the scope of the project. The work we report here is about understanding the existing annotation and ingesting it into an interoperable framework.

3 Some End User Goals

The goal of the AusNC is to bring together more collections of Australian language so that researchers can benefit from being able to work with many collections in a uniform way. To illustrate this we will look at two example 'use cases' from the point of view of a Linguistics researcher.

The first case involves a study of utterance final constructions and their effect on the following utterances. Researchers want to identify certain lexical items occurring at the end of a speaker turn (eg. 'is it?', 'can he?'), classify the turns according to the gender of the speaker and then study the turns and those that follow them to look for common patterns.

The second case looks at overlapping speech in dialogue. The researcher is interested in the lexical items that are used in backchannel interjections ('hmm', 'yeah', 'really') and so wants to generate a list of words that occur during overlapping speech ordered by frequency and distinguished by the gender of the speaker.

Each of these tasks can be achieved by researchers on the existing data sets; in fact they are things that have been done already. The main issue is that the variability in the way that meta-data and annotation is represented in the corpora mean that any study that wanted to work over multiple corpora would need to process each one separately with difficult and different manual methods. The three corpora that we'll target in these examples are the Griffith, Monash and ICE-AUS corpora, all of which contain transcriptions of dialogue with some overlap information and which have been identified by researchers as good resources that they would like to be able to make use of.

The two cases are similar in that they both involve identifying speaker turns in dialogue. These are represented differently in the source corpora, with Griffith and Monash using formatting within the Word or PDF document (a line starting with a speaker identifier and a colon) and ICE-AUS using XML like markup in the text. In Griffith and Monash, the end of a speaker turn is implicitly marked as the newline before the start of the next turn and so searching for words at the end of turns is problematic.

Speaker meta-data is available in all three corpora but in very different forms. In ICE-AUS it is in a separate spreadsheet; in Griffith and Monash it is at the head of each transcript in a table. Essentially, finding the gender of each speaker is a manual process of tabulating the available data, except for Monash which encodes gender in the speaker identifier.

The third kind of annotation we need to look at is overlap. This is handled very differently in each case. Monash and ICE-AUS use explicit markup for regions of overlapped speech - in the case of Monash the text is enclosed in square brackets. Griffith's CA style of annotation uses an open square bracket to mark the start of overlap and vertical alignment to mark the relationship between the two speaker's utterances, but the end of overlap is not marked explicitly. ICE-AUS has an explicit mechanism for linking two overlapping segments but Monash relies on the reader to line up multiple segments. So if we have three speakers:

```
BH4M:     [whats that]
BH4MMo:   [what] did he do?
BH4MFa:   .. well we were going to
          the milkbar on Sunday
BH4MMo:   [oh]
BH4M:     [oh] here we go
```

we need to be very careful to keep track of the overlaps from the start of the discourse to be able to identify what overlaps with what.

A final consideration is document selection. Both the Monash and Griffith corpora represent a single kind of language use - conversation. However, the ICE-AUS corpus contains samples of conversation alongside monologues, newspaper text and fiction. Clearly in carrying out any study over multiple corpora, a researcher needs to be able to select appropriate documents based on their descriptive meta-data.

Based on this review, it is clear that if a researcher is to be able to perform queries on more than one data set, the main thing standing in their way is the diversity of representations of the phenomena that are annotated. In this case, the meaning of the annotations is aligned in each case (speaker turns, overlap) but their realisation is quite distinct. In addition, the link to meta-data about the speaker and the kind of language represented in each document needs to be clear.

4 Technical Architecture

The goal of the project is to establish a unified technical platform that can store the source media (text, audio, video), meta-data and annotations from these different corpora and provide not only online access to the resources but value-added services that make them more useful to the research community. The technical architecture builds on the DADA system (Cassidy, 2010) and integrates separate data stores for the source media, meta-data and annotation behind a web based presentation and analysis layer based on the Plone content management system.

The meta-data and annotation stores are built on an RDF triple store. The use of RDF for meta-data is well understood and our implementation makes use of standard vocabularies as far as possible to describe corpora and their contents. Modelling annotation data as RDF is less well established but our earlier work has shown that the data model and query language are well suited to the task. Among the challenges in this project are managing the scale of data resulting from ingesting annotations from a large number of corpora and dealing with the issues that arise in storing many different corpora in a single annotation store.

4.1 Parsing Annotation

All annotation in the corpus is stored as stand-off annotation, so the source media, be it text, audio or video, is stored separately in a web accessible location that will be referenced by the meta-data and annotation stores. For audio and video resources this is standard practice; for the text based corpora this has meant generating markup-free versions of the text to act as the source media.

To generate the markup-free based versions of the text we have developed a parsing library that is able to handle the variety of markup that we have found in our target corpora. The library, based on the Python `pyparsing`[2] module, is written such that new parsers can be built by chaining together primitive parser elements. The output of the parsing process is twofold – the plain text without markup and a stream of annotation objects that reference character offsets in the plain text stream. An example of calling a simple parsing procedure is shown in Figure 1.

The output from these parsing procedures is combined to produce the plain text version of the document and a collection of annotations that are then converted to RDF.

In the case of the ICE corpus, we drew on earlier work on a validating parser for ICE markup (Wong et al., 2011) which was able to convert the validated ICE markup to a standoff annotation format suitable

[2] `http://pyparsing.wikispaces.com/`

```
>>> markupParser('h', 'heading').parseString("<h>some stuff</h>")
([@(some stuff,[heading:  0 -> 10])], {})
```

Figure 1: An example call to one of the parser procedures, in this case parsing an XML style header from the ACE corpus. The result is a representation of the plain text and the annotation with character offsets.

```
RF3:   [Okay]
BH1M:  [Im fifteen] years old.
RF3:   Fifteen?
BH1M:  Yes.
RF3:   How do I spell your surname?
```

Figure 2: Sample of the original text from the Monash corpus

```
Okay
Im fifteen years old.
Fifteen?
Yes.
How do I spell your surname?
```

Figure 3: Sample of plain text from the Monash corpus corresponding to the raw text in Figure 2

```
monash:speaker/BH1M a foaf:Person;
    monashp:role "primary";
    monashp:school "BH";
    foaf:age "15";
    foaf:gender "male" .
```

Figure 4: Part of the meta-data for the sample of Figure 2 describing the speaker BH1M.

for ingestion.

As described in earlier papers on the DADA system (Cassidy, 2010), annotations are modelled as RDF and stored on the server in a Sesame triple store. The annotation model used is now closely aligned with the proposed ISO Linguistic Annotation Framework (ISO 24612, 2012) and the intention is that this system is a realisation of that standard as an annotation database, rather than a data exchange format.

4.2 Parsing Speaker Turns and Overlaps

An example of the text version of a document from the Monash corpus is shown in Figure 2; this contains examples of both of the phenomena mentioned in Section 3: speaker turns and overlap. The parsing process removes all markup (in this case, the speaker identifiers and the square bracket overlap notation) and generates the text shown in Figure 3 and a collection of RDF annotations which will be discussed below.

A second part of the ingestion process is to read and normalise the meta-data that is associated with the primary data. This is found in different forms: spreadsheets, text files and in the case of the Monash and Griffith corpora, in tables at the start of each transcription file. This data is parsed as part of processing the document and normalised to standard vocabularies where possible. Items like speaker identifiers are treated specially to ensure we maintain the link between speaker data and annotations on speaker turns, and that speaker identifiers are unique across the different corpora. Figure 4 shows the description of one speaker which uses the standard `foaf` namespace[3] commonly used to describe individuals. Since the same property names are always used, we can filter speakers by gender or age (where available) irrespective of the corpus they contributed to.

A sample speaker turn annotation is shown in Figure 5 in the RDF format used by the DADA system. This is basically a set of descriptions of objects via attribute-value pairs. In this case, the object `monash:5514A` is an instance of the class `dada:Annotation` and has properties `dada:type` etc. The colon notation denotes namespaced identifiers which can be described by a formal vocabulary (ontology). The RDF descriptions of annotations can reference parts of the metadata as seen in the `ausnc:speakerid` property in the example which references the speaker described in Figure 4.

The text in Figure 2 also contains an example of overlapping speech marked as square bracketed text. This is also recognised as part of the parsing process

[3]`http://www.foaf-project.org/`

```
monash:5514A a dada:Annotation;
    dada:type ausnc:speaker;
    dada:partof monash:10cdaedc;
    dada:targets monash:5514L;
    ausnc:speakerid monash:speaker/BH1M .

monash:5514L a dada:UTF8Region;
    dada:start 91;
    dada:end 113 .
```

Figure 5: Part of the RDF annotation generated from the raw text in Figure 2. The first part describes the annotation object itself which has a number of properties, this *targets* a locator object described in the second part as a region bounded by UTF8 character offsets. This represents the second line in Figure 2.

```
monash:5513A a dada:Annotation;
    dada:type ausnc:overlap;
    dada:partof monash:10cdaedc;
    dada:targets monash:5513L .

monash:5513L a dada:UTF8Region;
    dada:start 91;
    dada:end 102 .
```

Figure 6: Part of the RDF annotation generated from the raw text in Figure 2 showing an overlap annotation corresponding to the text 'Im Fifteen'

and annotations marking this region as overlap are generated. In this case it would be useful to also record the relationship between these two instances of overlap - that 'Okay' is spoken at the same time as 'Im Fifteen'; however, our parser is not yet capable of doing this for the Monash data. We have done this for another corpus, ICE-AUS as part of the work reported in (Wong et al., 2011) but in this case, instances of overlap were numbered to allow the correspondence to be made explicit. However, we found that since the annotators were unable to validate the markup they were writing (it was XML like but didn't conform to any formal system), there were many deviations from the stated rules that needed to be corrected before a useable parse could be completed. We suspect that this will be the case with the Monash data as well.

There are also examples of overlap in the Griffith corpus, marked up with the CA convention of an open square bracket, vertically aligned with the corresponding text from the second speaker. Here's an example:

```
11  H:  [family gen[der book two
12  S:  [can-       [can I borrow
13      that?
```

Given the involvement of vertical alignment and the lack of explicit end markers for the overlap, we've not yet been able to successfully parse this markup, however we are confident that we should be able to recover most of the information here with further work.

5 Discussion

5.1 Achieving User Goals

In Section 3 we presented two example tasks that users had identified as targets for the work we were doing in building the AusNC. These relied on having a more uniform annotation model that would allow queries over speaker turns and overlapping speech when the source corpora have quite different ways of expressing this markup.

We have described the ingest process for the AusNC which aims to build this uniform representation of annotation. An important part of this is the use of common labels for annotation types such that the same phenomena in different corpora can be identified in the same way. While the examples we chose were quite simple (and not particularly 'semantic'), they illustrate the concept of using standard types to describe kinds of annotation.

The solution that we have describe only goes part of the way towards solving the problems presented in Section 3 however. We've built a model but we need to build the query tools and analysis engines that can make use of the data to answer questions from researchers. We are currently involved in a follow-on project that aims to do just this, adding infrastructure for running tools that will support query and analysis of corpus data from the AusNC as well as generating new annotations by running automatic processes such as parser and POS taggers.

5.2 Annotation Types

Though the annotation data model is standardised across the different corpora, the types and contents of the annotations is different. The `dada:type` property of each annotation denotes an *annotation type* while the `ausnc:val` property is used to carry a value or label for the annotation. Other feature values can be expressed as additional RDF properties on the annotation node.

The concept of annotation type is not directly expressed in the ISO-LAF standard but is realised in most examples as a non-distinguished property of each annotation or via the AnnotationSpace property. The main point being that there is no *requirement* in ISO-LAF for any kind of type system but that there are a couple of mechanisms by which one could be implemented which would be equivalent to the model used here.

The use of the type system allows us to assert that certain kinds of annotation are semantically equivalent - in this case the speaker turns and overlaps in different corpora. This is a key to the interoperability of annotations because without this we cannot reliably treat the annotations as having the same meaning. The use of RDF makes it natural to use a schema to describe the annotation types, meaning that we can generate schemas to describe different styles of annotation - from transcribed dialogue to Penn Treebank style parse trees.

In order to make any type system useful, the way that it is used needs to be standardised. The DADA vocabulary makes one suggestion that is compatible with the ISO-LAF framework; while there may be other options to consider, it would be an important next step to discuss how this should be realised within the standard.

5.3 Other Annotation Types in AusNC

As the ingest scripts were developed for the different corpora in AusNC, common type names were used for annotations where possible. However, since the focus of the project was on the ingestion of primary data and meta-data, there were only a small number of types that were identified as common over more than one corpus.

In all other cases, annotation type names, values and other properties were derived from the names used in the individual corpora or where appropriate in the documentation for the corpora. A good example is the Griffith corpus which uses Conversational Analysis markup embedded in the text. The documentation for this annotation style was taken from (Lerner, 2004) which contains a glossary of transcription symbols with an informal description of their use and meaning. Table 1 lists the types that we have parsed with some examples of their use (there are a few other types that are used in the corpus that we are still working on parsing correctly).

Type Name	Example
micropause	(.)
pause	(1.2)
elongation	fo:r commu:nicating
intonation	if ↑I couldnt bo↓rrow,
latched-utterance	7 H: sexuality=
	8 S: =ah
speaker	5 S: I'm glad I saw you
volume	business °cause° I missed
uncertain	S: (,) this morning,

Table 1: Annotation types and examples from the Griffith corpus

6 Summary

This paper has tried to summarise some of our experiences in taking source data in many different formats and generating a single, interoperable annotation store that can hold annotations on many resources from different collections. The current system is able to present these resources via the web[4] and we are now starting to develop tools to work with the annotated data to help answer research questions for the diverse communities who make use of this data.

References

Steve Cassidy. 2010. An RDF Realisation of LAF in the DADA Annotation Server. In *Proceedings of ISA-5*, Hong Kong, January.

ISO 24612. 2012. Language Resource Management – Linguistic Annotation Framework.

G.H. Lerner. 2004. *Conversation analysis: studies from the first generation*. Pragmatics & beyond. John Benjamins Pub.

Deanna Wong, Steve Cassidy, and Pam Peters. 2011. Updating the ice annotation system: tagging, parsing and validation. *Corpora*, 6(2):115–144.

[4]`http://ausnc.org.au/`

Conceptual and Representational Choices in Defining an ISO Standard for Semantic Role Annotation

Harry Bunt
TiCC, Tilburg Center for
Cognition and Communication
Tilburg University,
Tilburg, The Netherlands
harry.bunt@uvt.nl

Martha Palmer
Department of Linguistics
University of Colorado
Boulder, Co.
USA
martha.palmer@colorado.edu

Abstract

This paper presents two elements of the ISO standard for semantic role annotation which is under development (ISO CD 24617-4:2013), namely (a) the metamodel, which describes the types of concepts that may occur in semantic role annotation and their conceptual relations, and (b) an annotation language for expressing semantic role annotations, with its abstract syntax, XML-based concrete syntax, and semantics.

1 Introduction

ISO project 24617-4, Language resource management Semantic annotation framework Part 4: Semantic Roles, has the aim of defining an international standard for the annotation of semantic roles, including an inventory of core semantic roles defined as ISO data categories, and an annotation language with an XML-based representation format and a formal semantics.

Semantic roles are receiving increasing interest in the information processing community because they make explicit the key conceptual relations of participation between a verb and its arguments, i.e., they specify Who did what to whom, and when, where, why, and how. For English alone, there are already several different semantic role frameworks, including FrameNet, VerbNet, LIRICS, EngVallex and PropBank (see Fillmore & Baker, 2004; Kipper-Schuler, 2005; Schiffrin & Bunt, 2007; EngVallex, 2011; and Palmer et al., 2005, respectively). Although these have been developed independently, there are strong underlying compatibilities between these frameworks, and they share a central definition of what a semantic role is, and what its span is, within an individual sentence. In addition to defining key concepts, the ISO standard aims at clarifying and specifying these underlying compatibilities and providing where possible a mapping between similar semantic roles across different frameworks. This mapping illustrates how different semantic role definitions can be linked to each other across frameworks, and presupposes a specification of clearly defined criteria for distinguishing semantic roles.

The specification can be used in two different situations:

- in annotations where the semantic roles are recorded in annotated corpora;
- as a dynamic structure produced by automatic systems; a process typically called semantic role labelling (SRL)

The objectives of this specification are to provide:

- A reference set of data categories defining a structured collection of semantic roles with an explicit semantics.
- A pivot representation based on a framework for defining semantic roles that could facilitate mapping between different formalisms (alternative semantic role representations/syntactic theories/eventually different languages) promoting interoperability.
- Guidelines for creating new resources that would be immediately interoperable with preexisting resources

The ISO semantic roles project follows a design strategy for semantic annotation projects that includes (a) the design of a conceptual model which contains the key concepts involved in the kind of semantic annotation and which describes how these concepts are related; such a model is called a 'metamodel' (see Bunt & Romary, 2004), and (b) the three-part definition of an annotation language, the parts being (1) an 'abstract syntax', specifying how the basic concepts defined by the metamodel may be combined into set-theoretic structures called annotation structures'; (2) a 'concrete syntax', defining a reference representation format, typically using XML, for representing the annotation structures defined by the abstract syntax, and (3) a formal semantics describing the meaning of annotation structures (see Bunt, 2010; 2013 for a description of this methodology, called the CASCADES methodology). This paper focuses primarily on the metamodel constructed in the project for semantic role annotation (section 2) and the definition of the annotation language (3). For a more detailed description of the frameworks discussed and of semantic roles in general see the ISO document ISO 24617-4:2013, Bonial et al. (2011) and Johnson et al. (2001). The paper concludes with a brief discussion of what has been achieved and what remains to be done.

2 A metamodel for semantic role annotation

2.1 Predicate-argument structures and eventualities

A predicative expression with its arguments can be viewed semantically as describing an actual or hypothetical eventuality with its participants. Associated with the predicate (most prototypically a verb) is a subcategorization frame, describing the participants that are expected in that particular type of eventuality. Each slot in the subcategorization frame can be given a semantic role label which can then be associated with any argument that fills that slot. In the most fine-grained view each individual lexical item can be seen as defining a unique eventuality type with a unique set of possible participants.

Different predicative expressions may share the same or a very similar set of possible participants. Obvious examples are nouns and adjectives that constitute derived forms of the same lexical item (*observe, observance, observer*). Other examples are *buy* and *sell*, and *give* and *receive*. Depending on the desired level of generalization, the grouping of lexical items into shared subcategorization frame classes may stop there (this is one view of the PropBank Frame Files) or may continue to include a small set of items with very closely related semantics (the FrameNet view) or may extend to include items that share specific patterns of argument types but may have a fairly tenuous semantic relation (the VerbNet view). These frameworks take the subcategorization frame as a whole into consideration when determining the choice of individual semantic roles; this is motivated by examples such as *replace*, which can have one participant as the old item being replaced and another participant as the new item replacing it, with an obvious dependency between these two roles.

LIRICS does not use subcategorization frames or any other a priori association of semantic roles, but uses a set of features, like intentionality of the involvement of a participant, to distinguish among individual semantic roles, in the spirit of Dowty (1991). For example, in (1a), the behaviour of 'Martin' is clearly intentional, and he would be assigned the Agent role. In (1b), there is no intentionality involved, and *The lightning* would be assigned the Cause role. Sentence (1c) is ambiguous as to whether Martin's behaviour caused the children to be frightened as an intended or as an unintended effect, and so the semantic role of *Martin's behaviour* is either Agent or Cause.

(1) a. Martin frightened the children by pulling faces at them.

b. The lightning frightened the children.

c. Martin's behaviour frightened the children.

Note that the same word can have multiple senses, each of which might be associated with a distinct event type, and therefore a distinct frame. In this case the word could be represented by several eventuality types, each one associated with a different frame or class. Therefore, for the approaches to semantic role labelling embodied in FrameNet, PropBank, EngVallex and VerbNet, there are three core elements that must be defined for semantic role labelling:

1. the word sense, or lexical unit, under consideration;
2. the frame associated with that word sense; and
3. specific semantic role labels associated with each slot in that frame that will be assigned to the participants filling the slot.

The more examples that can be provided to illustrate the degree of syntactic variation available to each sense, the better. These examples, or instances, are considered tokens that are each associated with the appropriate type definition.

An additional consideration in defining any semantic role labelling scheme is exactly which constituents are labeled as adjuncts and whether or not a set of general adjunct types is defined. It is notoriously hard to draw a clear line between arguments of a verb and adjuncts, and approaches to semantic role labelling differ in how they draw such a line, or finesse the question by giving individual labels to adjuncts associated with each eventuality type. Finally, frames may include information about likely semantic types of the semantic roles being specified.

The frames associated with a semantic role labelling scheme specify the roles associated with the eventuality types. (For FrameNet they would be the FrameNet Frames, for PropBank and for EngVallex they are the PropBank role sets or framesets, and for VerbNet they are defined in VerbNet classes.) The frames are typically consulted during annotation to guide the decisions and ensure consistency. This makes the specification of the frame a critical step in the path towards an annotated corpus. For each predicate in a language, a meta-level description of the predicate and its arguments needs to be created, with examples, which constitutes the definition of the eventuality type frame.

2.2 Eventualities, participants, types and tokens

Figure 1 visualizes the conceptual view that underlies semantic role annotation according to standard ISO 24617-4 under development. A predicative expression in natural language, in the sense in which it is understood in a given utterance, is viewed as denoting a certain type of eventuality, and the occurrence of the verb form in the utterance as denoting an instance (or 'token') of that type of eventuality. Each eventuality type has a semantic role set or 'frame' defined, which determines the possible choices of individual semantic roles for the participants in an instance of that eventuality type. Eventuality types may further be grouped into classes that have similar role sets, possibly defining hierarchies of event classes/types and the corresponding role sets/frames (not shown in Fig. 1).

Like eventualities, participants also have a semantic type, typically expressed by the lexical item that serves as the nominal head of a noun phrase or that forms the central element in a predicative expression. The metamodel in Fig. 1 indicates that in a given utterance, the semantic roles relate the participants that occurrences of nominal (or adverbial) lexical items refer to, to the eventualities corresponding to an occurrence of a verb (or noun, or other event-denoting predicative expression). Participants and eventualities are both tokens of certain types, which pertain to a semantic type system.

Since annotations add linguistic information to stretches of primary data, the identification of relevant stretches in the data is essential. In standoff format, this realized through pointers to the primary data (the original text) or to elements at another layer of annotation, such as a syntactic parse, where the regions of primary data are identified. Following ISO practice, the term *'markable'* is used to refer to the entities that anchor an annotation directly or indirectly in the primary data. Note that the metamodel stipulates that participants and eventualities are expressed by markables in the original text ('source document'), but that semantic roles are not textually expressed.

3 SemRolesML

3.1 Abstract syntax

The abstract syntax of an annotation language consists of two parts (Bunt, 2010): (a) a specification of the elements from which annotation structures are built up, called a 'conceptual inventory', and (b) a specification of the possible ways of combining these elements in set-theoretical structures, called 'annotation structures'.

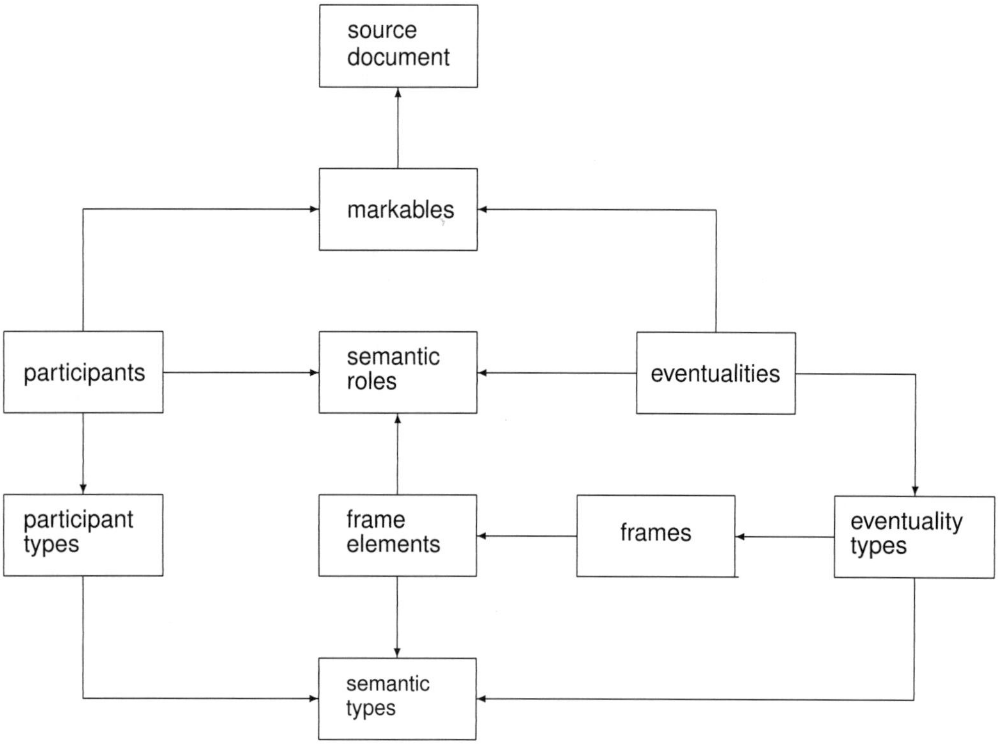

Figure 1: Metamodel for semantic role annotation.

a. Conceptual inventory

The conceptual inventory of the SemRoleML markup language, defined as part of ISO 24617-4, is derived from the metamodel shown in Fig. 1 by identifying among the categories of concepts in the metamodel those which are elementary and those which are composite, the latter being defined in terms of other concepts occurring in the metamodel. The listing of the basic concepts constitutes the conceptual inventory.

Of the ten categories represented in Fig. 1, the 'source document' is present only as a source of the markables and a carrier of possibly relevant metadata. Of the other nine categories, 'participants' and 'eventualities' are tokens of the basic concepts 'participant type' and 'eventuality type', respectively, and are identified by the occurrences of predicates and argument NPs in certain markables; as such they are instances (or 'tokens') of basic concepts, rather than basic concepts themselves. (Technically, they correspond to so-called 'entity structures' in the abstract syntax, see below.)

Concepts from the three categories at the bottom of Fig. 1, 'frames', 'frame elements' and 'semantic types', do not necessarily show up in semantic role annotations (but they often do in FrameNet annotations); they are especially important in the lexical resources supporting semantic role annotation. With respect to our abstract syntax, frames are a composite concept, that include n-tuples of frame elements. Frame elements include pairs of semantic role labels and specifications of the most likely semantic type of a participant playing that role, and are thus also composite concepts. So the five categories of elemenary concepts that form the SemRoleML conceptual inventory are: *markables, semantic roles, participant types, semantic types*, and *eventuality types*.

The specification of the SemRoleML conceptual inventory is thus the following listing of elementary concepts:

1. EV, a finite set of eventuality types, typically corresponding to verbs, nouns and adjectives.

2. RL, a finite set of semantic roles, such as the LIRICS role set (Schiffrin and Bunt, 2007; Petukhova and Bunt, 2007). This set can have a hierarchical organization, such as the unified VerbNet-LIRICS hierarchy presented by Bonial et al. (2011), with lower tiers expressing more fine-grained meanings, however this is not part of the conceptual inventory as such, but follows from the definitions of these roles (cf. Miltsakaki et al., 2008).

3. MA, a finite set of markables to which semantic roles can be attached.

4. PT, a finite set of participant types.

5. ST, a finite set of semantic types. The set PT of participant types and the set EV of eventuality types are subsets of ST.

b. Annotation Structures

An annotation structure is a set of entity structures and link structures. An entity structure is a pair $\langle m, s\rangle$ consisting of a markable (element of MA) and a specification of semantic information about that markable. For semantic role annotation, entity structures describe the eventualities and participants (both at token level) that are related by semantic roles. There are two kinds of entity structures in SemRoleML, those where the component s characterizes an eventuality and those where it characterizes a participant.

A link structure in SemRoleML is a triplet $\langle \epsilon_e, \epsilon_p, \rho\rangle$ consisting of two entity structures ϵ_e and ϵ_p, corresponding to an eventuality and a participant, respectively, and a semantic role specification ρ, which is either simply a semantic role label R or a pair $\langle \phi, R\rangle$, where ϕ is a frame, i.e. a list of frame elements $\phi = \langle \phi_1, \phi_2, \phi_k\rangle$. A frame element is either just a specification of a semantic role, or a pair $\langle R_i, t_i\rangle$ consisting of the specification of a semantic role and a semantic type (expected to subsume the participant type of a participant filling that role).

For the example sentence (2) two entity structures are created, one for the markable *The soprano*, and another one for the markable *sang*, shown in (3):

(2) The soprano sang

(3) a. $\epsilon_1 = \langle \textit{the soprano}, \text{SOPRANO}\rangle$
b. $\epsilon_2 = \langle \textit{sang}, \text{SING}\rangle$

For easy of readability, the strings *the soprano* and *sang* are used here to indicate markables (i.e. an occurrence of a stretch of text in the source document), SOPRANO is a participant type (an element of PT), and SING is an eventuality type (an element of EV).

A link structure is moreover created consisting of the two entity structures ϵ_1 and ϵ_2 and the semantic role *Agent*. The link structure is thus the triplet:

(4) $L_1 = \langle \epsilon_1, \epsilon_2, \textit{Agent}\rangle$

The annotation structure for sentence (2) is the pair consisting of these entity structures and link structure(s):

(5) $\alpha = \langle \{\epsilon_1, \epsilon_2\}, \{L_1\}\rangle$

Note that ST, the set of semantic types, can be used to distinguish semantic roles and help determine their applicability. These are specified as selectional preferences by VerbNet, and are often included in the textual descriptions in FrameNet. As with the semantic roles, inheritance relations can hold between semantic types; these can be based on an hierarchical classification such as the hypernyms in WordNet (Miller, 1990; Feelbaum, 1998). In the example *The soprano sang*, the verb *sing* will plausibly have a frame which specifies that the frame element for the Agent slot expects a participant with the semantic type ANIMATE (or maybe HUMAN $\cup$ BIRD, if we agree that only humans and birds sing); since sopranos are humans, the semantic type system should include the knowledge SOPRANO $\subset$ HUMAN, and therefore the participant type is indeed subsumed by the semantic type.

The frames discussed above specify for each eventuality type the associated set of semantic roles, and can be used to guide the annotation process. Each frame consists of an eventuality type, e (an element of EV), and a subset, S_e, of RL with at least one element, such that $e \in EV$, and $r_i \in RL$ for all $r_i \in S_e$. For example, the frame for *sing* as occurring in example (2) above would consist of the eventuality type, SING, and the possible roles, including *Agent* and *Theme*, both of which are members of RL.

3.2 Semantics

The CASCADES design methodology (Bunt, 2013), used in the development of ISO 246171-4, derives a formal semantics for a given abstract syntax through a translation of the components of annotation structures to discourse representation structures (DRSs, Kamp and Reyle, 1994), which are combined by unification operations into a DRS for the annotation structure as a whole.

An entity structure $\langle m, s \rangle$ is interpreted as a DRS which introduces a discourse marker paired with a name of the markable m,[1] and which contains for each component s_i of s a condition of the form $p_i(x, a_i)$, where a_i is the interpretation of the component s_i, p_i is a predicate that indicates the role of a_i, and x is the newly introduced discourse marker. So the entity structures ϵ_1 and ϵ_2 are interpreted as the following DRSs, where m_1 names the markable *the soprano* and m_2 the markable *sang*:

$$(6)\ \text{a. } \epsilon_1 \rightsquigarrow \begin{array}{|l|}\hline \langle m_1, x_1 \rangle \\ \hline \text{PARTICIP\_TYPE}(x_1, \textit{soprano}) \\ \hline \end{array}$$

$$\text{b. } \epsilon_2 \rightsquigarrow \begin{array}{|l|}\hline \langle m_2, e_1 \rangle \\ \hline \text{EVENT\_TYPE}(e_1, \textit{sing}) \\ \hline \end{array}$$

A link structure $\langle \langle m, s \rangle, \langle m', s' \rangle, \rho \rangle$ is interpreted as a DRS which introduces discourse markers z_1 and z_2, paired with the markables m and m', respectively, and which has a condition of the form $R'(z_1, z_2)$, where R' is the DRS-predicate interpreting the relation ρ.

So the link structure L_1 of (4) is interpreted as the following DRS:

$$(7)\ L_1 \rightsquigarrow \begin{array}{|l|}\hline \langle m_1, z_1 \rangle, \langle m_2, z_2 \rangle \\ \hline \text{AGENT}(z_1, z_2) \\ \hline \end{array}$$

Merging these interpretations of the entity and link structures results in the following interpretation of the annotation structure (5):

$$(8)\ \alpha \rightsquigarrow \begin{array}{|l|}\hline \langle m_1, x_1 \rangle, \langle m_2, e_1 \rangle \\ \hline \text{PARTICIP\_TYPE}(x_1, \textit{soprano}) \\ \text{EVENT\_TYPE}(e_1, \textit{sing}) \\ \text{AGENT}(e_1, x_1) \\ \hline \end{array}$$

Once the DRS-interpretations of the entity structures and link structure have been combined (see footnote 1), the markable names can be deleted, resulting in a DRS of the usual kind.

A classical DRS is semantically equivalent to a formula in first-order logic; in this case the equivalent formula is (9), which says that there exist an eventuality, an eventuality type, a participant, and a participant type, such that the eventuality is a token of the eventuality type, the participant is a token of that participant type, and the participant is the agent of the event.

$$(9)\ \exists e_1 . \exists et_1 . \exists p_1 . \exists pt_1 .\ \text{EVENT-TYPE}(e_1, et_1) \wedge \text{PART-TYPE}(p_1, pt_1) \wedge \text{AGENT}(e_1, p_1)$$

In this semantic representation, AGENT is a first-order predicate constant that expresses the meaning of the semantic role Agent. The hardest part of the semantics of SemRoleML is in fact the formal definition of the logical predicates that express the meanings of the individual semantic roles. Defining these predicates comes down to formalizing the semantic role definitions in ISO CD 24617-4: 2013, Annex A. Figure 1 shows three examples of these definition. The Agent role, for example, is defined as one where a participant initiates and carries out an event intentionally or consciously, and who exists independently of the event. The condition of acting 'intentionally or consciously' distinguishes the Agent role from the Cause role; the existence independently of the event forms one of the distinctions between the Agent and Cause roles on the one hand and the Result role on the other hand (and, more significantly, also distinguishes the Result role from the Theme and Patient roles).

The formalization of such definitions can be used to complete the semantics of semantic role annotations; for example, the interpretation (9) of the

[1] The paring of discourse markers with markable names serves to ensure that, when an annotated text is interpreted which contains more than one occurrence of the same stretch of text, the right occurrences are combined in the semantics. See Bunt (2012) for details.

SemRoleML annotation of the sentence *The soprano sang* can be completed by replacing the predicate AGENT by (10a). Similarly, the semantics of CAUSE can be described by (10b).

(10) a. AGENT = $\lambda e.\lambda x.$ [Intent-Init(x,e) $\vee$ Consc-Init(x,e)] $\wedge$ [Intent-Do(x,e) $\vee$ Consc-Do(x,e)] $\wedge$ Indep-Exist(x,e)

b. CAUSE = $\lambda e.\lambda x.$ Init(e) $\wedge$ $\neg$Intent-Init(x,e) $\wedge$ $\neg$Consc-Init(x,e) $\wedge$ $\neg$Intent-Do(x,e) $\wedge$ Indep-Exist(x,e)

For some frameworks this approach to the semantics of semantic roles could be almost prohibitively burdensome. FrameNet has thousands of frame elements, and while VerbNet has less than 30, the definitions of each one can change subtly from class to class. On the other hand, this is perhaps the only way to semantically make sense of these elements with a formal rigour, required for automatic inferencing.

3.3 Concrete syntax

Following the CASCADES design methodology,a reference representation format for annotation structures, based on XML, can be defined as follows, given an abstract syntax specification.

1. For each element of the conceptual vocabulary define an XML name;
2. For each type of entity structure $\langle m, s\rangle$ define an XML element with the following attributes and values:
   (a) the special attribute `@xml:id`, whose value is an identifier of the entity structure representation;
   (b) the special attribute `@target`, whose value represents the markable m;
   (c) attributes whose values represent the components of s, and which themselves represent the significance of the components;
   (d) if s_i is an elementary concept then it is represented by its name.
3. For each type of link structure $\langle \epsilon_1, \epsilon_2, \rho\rangle$ define an XML element with three attributes, two which have values that refer to the representations of the entity structures ϵ_1 and ϵ_2, the value of the third denoting the semantic relation between them.
4. For each type of auxiliary structure (see below) specify an XML representation.

Applied to the abstract syntax of SemRoleML, this results in the following concrete syntax:

1. The XML elements `<event>` and `<participant>` are defined for representing entity structures corresponding to eventualities and participants, respectively. Both of these elements have the attributes `@xml:id` and `@target`, and additionally they have the attributes `@eventType` and `@participantType`, respectively.
2. XML constants are chosen for the values of the attributes `@eventType` and `@participantType`.
3. The XML element `<srLink>` is defined for representing semantic role link structures; this element has the attributes `@event` and `@participant` whose values refer to the eventuality and the participant that are related by a semantic role, and the attribute `@semRole` whose value represents the semantic role of the participant in the eventuality.
4. For completeness, we mention that it is convenient to introduce auxiliary structures in the abstract syntax for frames and frame elements, which may occur within the relational component ρ of a link structure $\langle \epsilon_e, \epsilon_p, \rho\rangle$; see ISO CD 24617-4 (2013) for more details.

For the example sentence *The soprano sang* this gives us the following representation of the annotation structure (5):

(11)

```
<event xml:id="e1"
 target="#m2"
 eventType="sing"/>
<participant xml:id="x1"
 target="#m1"
 participantType="soprano"/>
<srLink event="#e1"
 participant="#x1"
 semRole="agent"/>
```

/agent/	
Definition	Participant in an event who initiates and carries out the event intentionally or consciously, and who exists independently of the event.
– Source	Adapted from Dowty [1989], EAGLES, SIL, Sowa [2000] and UNL
Explanation	An agent may be animate, or only seemingly, or perceived, as animate; this is so that cases of nonhuman agency such as a robot, or an institution will not be excluded from being able to initiate an event, e.g. "GM offers rebates on its new models".
Example	"John [agent e1] built e1 the house"

/cause/	
Definition	Participant in an event that initiates the event, but that does not act with any intentionality or consciousness; the participant exists independently of the event.
– Source	Adapted from: SIL (Causer) and Sowa [2000] (Effector)
Explanation	Except for the lack of intentionality of the participant, this semantic role is very similar to that of the agent and in fact shares all its other properties. The role of cause can often be identified with verbs of initiation, or causation, such as: to cause, to produce, to start, to originate, to occasion, to generate.
Example	"The wind [cause e1] broke e1 the window" "His talk [cause e1] produced e1 a violent reaction e2 from the crow

/result/	
Definition	Participant in an event that comes into existence through the event. It indicates a terminal point for the event: when it is reached, then the event does not continue.
– Source	Adapted from Sowa [2000]
Explanation	Result is the completed point of a process, and unlike goal is dependent upon the event for its existence.
Example	"(Within the past two months [duration e1]) (a bomb [cause e1]) exploded e1 (in the offices of El Espectador in Bogota [location e1]), (destroying e2 (a major part of its installations and equipment [patient e2]) [result e1])"

Figure 2: Examples of LIRICS semantic role definitions in the form of ISO data categories (from Schiffrin & Bunt, 2007)

4 Conclusion

In this paper we have described a number of fundamental decisions in the process of defining an international ISO standard for the annotation of semantic roles. Starting from the conceptual view of predication in natural language as referring to (actual or hypothetical) eventualities and their participants, and of semantic roles as ways in which a participant may be involved in an eventuality, we outlined a metamodel which specifies the categories of basic concepts involved in semantic role annotation, and which shows how these concepts are interrelated. We subsequently defined an annotation language, SemRoleML, which has an XML-based pivot representation format for semantic role annotations, and a semantics that is defined for an abstract syntax that underlies these representations. We showed how the formalization of semantic role definitions can in principle be the basis of a semantics of semantic role annotations.

Two advantages of defining the semantic role annotation language SemRoleML in this way, following the CASCADES methodology of defining semantic annotations, are

(1) that different representation formats, used to encode the same underlying abstract structures,

share the same semantics, and are thus semantically interoperable;

(2) that integration of the annotation of semantic roles with the annotation of other types of semantic information, such as information about time and events according to ISO 24617-1, or about spatial information (ISO 24617-7, under development) or about discourse relations (ISO 24617-8, under developent) is facilitated, since these all follow the same design methodology;

(3) that annotations of other linguistic phenomena, especially when following the ISO Linguistic Annotation Framework (ISO 24613:2012), such as annotations of syntactic, pragmatic and contextual information, can be combined with semantic role annotations; many of these are helpful and sometimes even necessary to determine word senses and resolve references for the automatic recognition of semantic roles.

All this helps to make these annotation schemes mutually interoperable and combinable.

Important work that remains to be done is the formalization of all the semantic role definitions which are included in ISO CD 24617-4, including the specification of meaning postulates for the predicates used in their interpretation, in order to fully specify the inferences that may be drawn from the semantic roles used in an annotated corpus.

References

Bonial, Claire, William Corvey, Volha Petukhova, Martha Palmer, and Harry Bunt (2011) A Hierarchical Unification of LIRICS and VerbNet Thematic Roles, in *Proceedings ICSC Workshop on Semantic Annotation for Computational Linguistic Resources (SACL-ISCS 2011)*, September 21, 2011, Stanford, CA.

Bunt, Harry (2010) A Methodology for designing semantic annotation languages exploiting syntactic-semantic iso-morphisms. In: Alex Fang, Nancy Ide, and Jonathan Webber (eds.) *Proceedings ICGL 2010, the 2nd International Conference on Global Interoperability for Language Resources*, Hong Kong, pp. 29–45.

Bunt, Harry (2012) Annotations that effectively contribute to semantic interpretation. Forthcoming in Harry Bunt, Johan Bos and Stephen Pulman (eds) *Computing Meaning, Vol. 4*. Springer, Berlin.

Bunt, Harry (2013) A methodology for designing semantic annotations. Forthcoming in *Language Resources and Evaluation.*

Bunt, Harry and Laurent Romary (2004) Standardization in Multimodal Content Representation: Some Methodological Issues. In *Proceedings LREC 2004*, Lisbon, pp. 2219-2222.

Dowty. David (1991) Thematic Proto-Roles and Argument Selection. *Language*, 67:547-619.

EngVallex 2011 Charles University in Prague. Available at (Accessed 9/10/2012): http://ufal.mff.cuni.cz/lindat/EngVallex.html

Fellbaum, Christiane (1998) *WordNet: An Electronic Lexical Data-base. Language, Speech and Communications.* MIT Press, Cambridge, MA.

Fillmore, Charles; Collin Baker, and Hiroaki Sato (2004). FrameNet as a "Net". In *Proceedings 4th International Conference on Language Resources and Evaluation (LREC 2004)*, pp. 1091-1094

ISO 24612:2012 Language Resource Management - Linguistic Annotation Framework. Spring 2012. ISO, Geneva.

ISO 24617-1:2012 Language Resource Management - Semantic Annotation Framework, Part 1: Time and events. ISO International Standard, Spring 2012. ISO, Geneva.

ISO CD 24617-4:2013 Language Resource Management - Semantic Annotation Framework, Part 4: Semantic roles. ISO Committee Draft, March 2013. ISO, Geneva.

Johnson, Christopher R., Charles J. Fillmore, Esther J.Wood, Josef Ruppenhofer, Margaret Urban, Miriam R. L. Petruck, and Collin F. Baker, 2001. The FrameNet Project: Tools for Lexicon Building. Unpublished Report, University of Berkeley.

Kamp, Hans and Uwe Reyle, (1993) From discourse to logic. Kluwer, Dordrecht.

Kipper-Schuler, Karin. 2005. VerbNet: A Broad-Coverage, Comprehensive Verb Lexicon. Ph.D. Thesis,University of Pennsylvania.

Miller, George A., 1990, WordNet: An on-line lexical database. *International Journal of Lexicography* 3(4) pp. 235312

Miltsakaki, Eleni, Livio Robaldi, Alan Lee and Aravind Joshi (2008) Sense Annotation in the Penn Discourse Treebank. In *Computational Linguistics and Intelligent Text Processing*, Lecture Notes in Computer Science Vol. 4919. Springer, Berlin, pp. 275-286.

Palmer, Martha, Daniel Gildea, and Paul Kingsbury. 2005. The Proposition Bank:An Annotated Corpus of Semantic Roles. *Computational Linguistics*, 31(1):71106.

Petukhova, Volha, Harry Bunt and Amanda Schiffrin (2007) LIRICS semantic role annotation: Design and evaluation of a set of data categories. In *Proceedings 6th International Conference on Language Resources and Evaluation (LREC 2008)*, Marrakech.

Schiffrin, Amanda and Harry Bunt. 2007. LIRICS Deliverable D4.3. Documented compilation of semantic data categories. `http://lirics.loria.fr`.

Veridicity annotation in the lexicon? A look at factive adjectives

Annie Zaenen
CSLI / Stanford University
azaenen@stanford.edu

Lauri Karttunen
CSLI / Stanford University
laurik@stanford.edu

Abstract

In this note, we look at the factors that influence veridicity judgments with factive predicates. We show that more context factors play a role than is generally assumed. We propose to use crowd sourcing techniques to understand these factors better and briefly discuss the consequences for the association of lexical signatures with items in the lexicon.

1 Veridicity: what and why

Recognizing the inferential properties of constructions and of lexical items is important for NLU (Natural Language Understanding) systems. In this paper we look at FACTUAL INFERENCES, inferences that allow the reader to conclude that an event has happened or will happen or that a state of affairs pertains or will pertain. We will refer to events and states together as SOAs. Factuality is in the world and outside of the text. In cases where the reader has no direct perceptual knowledge about the SOAs, she has to evaluate the factuality of a SOA referred to in a text based on her decoding of the author's representation of the factuality of the SOA and on her knowledge about the world and about the author's reliability. Authors have a plethora of means to signal whether they want to present SOAs as factual, as having happened or going to happen or as being more or less probable, possible, unlikely or not factual at all. We will call this presentation of a SOA the VERIDICITY of a SOA. We will call the reader's interpretation of the author's intention, the RIV (READER INFERRED VERIDICITY) and the reader judgment about the factuality of a SOA, RIF (READER INFERRED FACTUALITY).

Annotation can, at its best, only provide us with RIVs as the author is typically not available for consultation. This leads to a methodological problem. A reader will in his interpretation of a sentence be sensitive, not only to the way an author signals her intentions but also to what he knows about the world. To circumvent this problem as much as possible, corpus annotation for veridicity is typically done by trained annotators with extensive guidelines (see e.g. (Saurí, 2008), (Saurí and Pustejovsky, 2012)) but corpus annotation by trained annotators is an expensive enterprise, hence looks at a limited number of cases. For instance, to anticipate on a case we will discuss later in the paper, *lucky* occurs only once in the FactBank ((Saurí and Pustejovsky, 2009). Given that annotation is done on running text, it is also difficult to avoid that the reader's evaluation of the wider extralinguistic context might still play a role. We propose to supplement corpus annotation with crowd sourcing experiments. In these, sentences are presented to Mechanical Turk workers in limited contexts, very similar to the contexts in which linguists judge the effect of the contribution of a lexical item or a construction. But contrary to linguistic practice, we derive our examples from really occurring ones culled from the web and, more importantly, present them to many native speakers (typically 100) and in different variations to explore factors that can influence the interpretation. This kind of variation is very difficult to find in naturally occurring corpora of the type that are used for annotations (e.g. FactBank). This type of study complements the corpus studies in controlling the variation in the environment and in minimizing the external factors. With these experiments we intend to isolate a lexical signature for the lexical items we are interested in, in contradistinction to the interpretation in context that is provided by corpus annotation. It is, however, not intended to replace corpus studies because it has the drawback of not being able to take into account the influence of a wider linguistic environment.

2 Subclasses of veridical phenomena

The means an author uses to signal the factuality status of a SOA can be syntactic and/or lexical. Examples of syntactic means that have been exploited in textual inferencing tasks are appositives. They typically contain presupposed material and are in general factive. For a theoretical discussion of syntactically presupposed material see (Potts, 2005). Here we look at lexical sources of veridicity. They can be subdivided in IMPLICATIVE, FACTIVE and EPISTEMIC MODAL predicates. In all cases a lexical item occurs in the matrix clause of a syntactic frame where the embedded clause refers to a SOA. The veridicity status of the embedded clause is considered to be triggered by the lexical item, in the case of implicatives because there is an entailment-type relation, in the case of factives because there is a presupposition and in the case of epistemic modals because the embedded clause is under the scope of the modal.

(Karttunen, 1971; Karttunen, 2012) has studied several classes of IMPLICATIVE verbs and verb-noun collocations. Implicative constructions yield entailments about the veridicity of a complement clause. The entailment may be positive (+1) or negative (-1) depending on the polarity of the containing clause. Examples are:

(1) a. John managed to get the job done. (implies that the job got done)

b. John didn't manage to get the job done. (implies that the job did not get done)

c. John forgot to do the job. (implies that the job did not get done)

d. John didn't forget to do the job. (implies that the job got done)

There are several different inference patterns described in detail in the references given above. The polarity computation must take into account the many ways of expressing negation by particles (*not*), adverbs (*never*, *almost*), quantifiers (*no one*) and counterfactual mood as in (2).

(2) a. Rand Paul would have fired Clinton.

b. I wish I had been there.

FACTIVES were first studied (Kiparsky and Kiparsky, 1970). Their use indicates that the author considers the material in the embedded clause as presupposed (see e.g. (Beaver, 2010) for a discussion of relevant aspects of theories of presupposition). For the purpose of NLU, their most important characteristic is that their veridicity status does not change under negation or questioning ((Karttunen, 1971).

(3) a. It is annoying that people post stuff that no one cares about.

b. It isn't annoying that people post stuff that no one cares about.

c. Is it annoying that people post stuff that no one cares about?

Many implicative verbs are also presupposition triggers. For example, (1c) and (1d) both presuppose that John intended to do the job but carry opposite implications about whether the job got done. job The class of lexical items that express EPISTEMIC MODALITY includes verbs such as *must, have to, ought to, should, may, might*, adjectives such as *certain, likely, possible* and adverbs *certainly, likely, possibly*. There is a rich literature on this topic (Palmer, 2001; Kratzer, 2012).

With respect to veridicality, the most striking aspect of modal assertions is that even the *necessity* modals such as *must* and *have to* involve a weaker author commitment than the corresponding statements without the modal. An author who says

(4) It must be raining.

indicates that she has reasons to conclude that it is raining although she is not herself a witness to the event. A man who sees drops of water falling from the sky and recognizes it as rain would say *It is raining*; it would be odd for him to say (4). Direct evidence trumps reasoning.

The *possibility* modals such as *may* also indicate an inference or a guess that is made in the absence of direct evidence. The author of

(5) It may be raining.

indicates that she has no direct knowledge of whether it is raining but that conclusion is consistent with the evidence she has, but so is *it might not be raining*.

As epistemic modals show, author commitment to the veridicality of a SOA is a matter of degree ranging from *definitely true* to *definitely false* through a scale of weaker stances: *must, have to – probably, likely – possibly, perhaps, may – possibly not, perhaps not – probably not, most likely not – must not*.

Epistemic weakening applies to implications but not to presuppositions.

(6) John may have forgotten to do the job.

implies that the it is possible that John did not do the job but commits the author to the view, just as strongly as (1c) and (1d), that John had the intention to do the job. Presuppositions tend to "project" out of the embedded clauses that express them.

3 Annotating veridicity in the lexicon

Given the description above, one might come away with the idea that the only thing that needs to be done is to mark the veridical predicates in the lexicon and then have the system transmit a veridicity mark to the embedded clause. The mark would be different for the three classes as it would need to be sensitive to negation in different ways and the commitment might be absolute (negative or positive) or relative but the calculation would only have to look at one level of embedding. As the implementations discussed in (Nairn et al., 2006) and (MacCartney and Manning, 2009) show, the situation is quite a bit more complex. For factives specifically, we need to take into account what is known as the projection problem (Langendoen and Savin, 1971; Karttunen, 1974). But even if one assumes the projection problem solved, the picture is quite a bit more complicated than the short description in the previous section would let us to assume. We look in more detail at the complications that one finds with factive adjectives.

4 Factive adjectives

A great number of adjectives have been classified as factive in one or more of the following syntactic environments (see (Norrick, 1978) for the most extensive study that we are aware of):

(7) a. it be ADJ that S: It is annoying that he left early.

b. it be ADJ (for NP or of NP) to VP: It was daring for John to climb on the roof.

c. NP be ADJ that S: John is happy that the work got done.

d. NP be ADJ to VP: John was happy to get his paycheck.[1]

(7a) and (7b) are extraposition constructions, so there are also non-extraposed variants but as they are rare we leave them out of consideration here. We counted about 800 adjectives taking the (7a) construction, a slightly smaller number is supposed to occur in the (7b) one. Note that the syntactic frames themselves are not specific to factive adjectives. We can find non-factive adjectives in exactly the same syntactic environments:

(8) a. It is probable that he left early.

b. It is unlikely for John to come early.

c. He is certain that it will rain.

d. He is likely to come early.

4.1 Problem 1: variation

The first problem that arises is that when one looks at the data available on the web: several of these adjectives are used as non-factive implicatives in the construction in (7d), as we can see from the following examples (simplified from web examples):

[1] Constructions with -ing forms are also possible. We leave them out of the picture here because they have not been studied systematically.

(9) a. This is my first trip to Italy, so I was not brave to venture out alone.

b. Luckily, she was not stupid to send them any money.

c. He was not stupid to think she would remain the same weak little girl.

d. It was raining and snowing like crazy in March here, so I was not stupid to risk the customer car, my license and my life.

e. She still was not brave to approach the cars, even the couple of cars right in front of her.

f. I was not lucky to have a good view.

The intended meaning of these sentences is clear but are the implicative interpretations of these sentences available to all speakers or are they just the creation of netizens whose command of English is weak or are they part of a bona fide unrecognized variant of English?

4.2 Problem 2: context[2]

As explained above, the received wisdom is that the factors that determine the inferential properties of a lexical item are the lexical item itself and its syntactic frame. The syntactic frame is in general meant to refer to a loose notion of subcategorization[3]. It consists of the environment of the item expressed in terms of syntactic categories, be it Phrase Structure categories or Dependency Grammar ones. This is the approach taken in VerbNet (Kipper-Schuler, 2005), where some semantic frames are associated with Phrase Structure syntactic frames, giving it a potential basis to make some inferential properties explicit. We work here too with Phrase Structure categories because most of the preceding literature on adjectives is in Phrase Structure terms. Under such an approach, we would list the adjectives that can be found in the frames given above in (7) and associate the factivity marker with them in case they are factive and different marker in case they are not. But both introspection and experimental studies will tell us that this is not sufficient. Consider the following pair:

(10) a. It was fool hearted of John to go on a trip around the world.

b. It is fool hearted to go on a trip around the world.

(10a) will indeed get a factive interpretation but (10b) will not.

4.3 Crowd sourcing for RIVs

The two problems above convinced us that, before proposing an veridicity annotation scheme for lexical items, we should study variation and context in more detail. To do this, we set up several Mechanical Turk experiments. In one, we presented Mechanical Turk workers with sentences like those in (9) (not including 9f) asking them both about how they understood them and whether they would use them to express the interpretation they had given. The preliminary results show that most speakers indeed interpret the sentences as implicating that the embedded clause is false but, more importantly, this non-factive interpretation was considered unobjectionable by 20% of native users of English (we controlled for this by asking the MT workers explicitly about their command of English ("Was English the primary language you used in ...") and by asking them to judge sentences that any native speaker of English would get right). 20% seems to be a large minority to ignore.

For the one adjective that we have studied in detail, *lucky*, the native speakers that consider examples such as (9f) as ill-formed and would require an *enough* to get the intended interpretation are in the minority according to an informal survey we did in parallel with the MT study. This suggests that the split between users accepting the implicative interpretation and those that don't might not be the same for each adjective.

With respect to the examples in (9), we presented the MT workers with several variants: tense variation (past/present) and three different subject conditions (specific subject, non specific but explicit sub-

[2]The problem we discuss here for adjectives is discussed in a more theoretical setting for verbs by (Beaver, 2010)

[3]It is a loose notion because some elements that are recognized as part of the frame might reconsidered adjuncts rather than arguments in a strict syntactic sense. We do not go into this debate here as the distinction between arguments and adjuncts is often rather difficult to draw.

ject and no subject), as well as the difference between *of* and *for* PPs as illustrated below:

(11) a. It was fool hearted of John to go on a trip around the world.

b. It was fool hearted of old people to go on a trip around the world.

c. It was fool hearted for John to go on a trip around the world.

d. It was fool hearted for old people to go on a trip around the world.

e. It was fool hearted to go on a trip around the world.

f. It is fool hearted of John to go on a trip around the world.

g. It is fool hearted of old people to go on a trip around the world.

h. It is fool hearted for John to go on a trip around the world.

i. It is fool hearted for old people to go on a trip around the world.

j. It is fool hearted to go on a trip around the world.

We haven't yet analyzed the results in detail but only 4 Turkers out of 10 rated (11j) as having happened whereas 9 out of 10 found (11a) to be factual. There is no study of what is going on here but theoretical linguists wouldn't be too upset about the facts observed and invoke something like generic readings to account for the difference. From our more practical point of view, we observe that having an explicit subject and being in the past tense makes a difference. We need further studies to determine what the importance of various factors is.

The insufficiency of the syntactic frame information is illustrated even more dramatically with *lucky*. Here the use of the future tense changes the interpretation dramatically. Whereas in the past tense, *lucky* behaves as a factive or implicative adjective (see above), in the future it can have an idiomatic meaning illustrated in

(12) Wong Kwan will be lucky to break even. (from theFactBank (Saurí and Pustejovsky, 2009))

Here the speaker expresses the opinion that it is unlikely that Wong Kwan will break even. This idiomatic meaning seems to be the meaning that is predominant with the future tense but, unfortunately for annotation purposes, it is not the only possible one (see (Karttunen, 2013) for more details on *lucky*):

(13) Sooner or later, a drug company will be lucky to find such a molecule.

It is clear then that there are several factors beyond the syntactic frame as generally understood that play a role in determining the inferences of lexical items.

This situation is not specific to adjectives. Factive verbs have been studied in some detail and it has been noticed that, for some of them, the veridicity status depends on factors such as the person of the matrix clause. The most recent study that we are aware of is (Beaver, 2010) from which we the following examples.

(14) a. He is not aware that Morris saw the letter.

b. I am not aware that he [Morris] saw the Daschle letter. (CNN, November 2001, taken from (Beaver, 2010))

Whereas in the a-example, the embedded clause seems factual, this is not the case in the b-example. (Beaver, 2010), however, also gives examples of third person use where the factive presupposition is cancelled:

(15) Mrs London is not AWARE that there have ever been signs erected to stop use of the route, nor that there has ever been any obstruction to stop use of the route. (County Environment Director, Definitive Map Review 1996/2000, Public Rights of Way Committee, Parish of Aveton Gifford, 2000)

Another well-known environment that influences the status of factives is the antecedent of a conditional. The case of first person cancellation has been known for a long time. The third person case in mainly documented in (Beaver, 2010).

(16) a. If I REALIZE later that I have not told the truth, I will confess it to everyone.

b. If anyone DISCOVERS that one of our volunteers is charging money for being a volunteer, please notify me ASAP.(Tom Elliott, GenWeb, Waldo County, Maine, 30 Nov., 2000, taken from (Beaver, 2010))

4.4 What can be done with lexical signatures?

Lexicon annotation practice tends to take the lexical item into account and the syntactic frame. The data above suggests that much more needs to be taken into account, even in experimental settings that mimic that of linguistic introspection. The existence of variation shows that we have to allow for ambiguities in inference patterns, even when there are no detected meaning differences and the syntactic frames, as usually understood, are the same. The data in section 4.2 suggests two possible approaches: we could try to encode more specific patterns or we could base the attribution of a feature such as +factive on a 'prototypical environment', the kind of environment linguists have assumed tacitly. The first approach would most likely lead to an unmanageable explosion of frames. The second approach makes features such as +factive conditional; contrary to linguistic practice it is important to spell out the exact conditions in which they are supposed to hold. Further study of IMPLICATIVES and EPISTEMIC MODALS will most likely lead to similar conclusions.

Is it, however, possible to spell out these conditions? In what precedes we have talked as if the variation that we observe is due to morpho-syntactic factors such as tense. But providing more context, it is of course also perfectly possible to have generic interpretations, not implying factuality, with factive adjectives in the past as the following example illustrates:

(17) In the Middle Ages it was daring to express anything except orthodox opinions.

And again, although the idiomatic meaning of *lucky* occurs mainly with the future tense, one can find it in the past with non specific subjects:

(18) Just a hundred years ago a man was lucky to live to be 45.

The real conditioning factors that determine these interpretations are not morphological or syntactic; they are themselves semantic: it is not tense per se that influences the interpretation of *lucky* or of factive adjective complements, it is a form of genericity. There is no way that, in the current state of affairs, we can detect genericity directly.

Beaver concludes his corpus study stating

> I doubt that there is any general principle that would enable one to predict from the written form of an arbitrary sentence involving a cognitive factive whether the factive complement is presupposed by the author. Certainly, there is a tendency for the complement to be presupposed. And certainly there are types of sentence involving cognitive factives, notably in the first and second person, for which the complement is rarely if ever presupposed. But the grey area, the range of cases for which no small set of formal features of the text would tell you whether the complement is presupposed or not, is just too big.

This conclusion, however, is not very satisfying from a computational point of view. Whereas the situation might be complex, there is a need for approaches that are more sophisticated than the one described in the beginning of this section but less defeatist than Beaver's[4]. We will continue to run into this unsatisfactory situation as long as we don't have systems that can directly couple NLU to real world experiences. At this point we have to work with morphological and syntactic proxies. Past tense, for instance, is a good proxy for episodical as distinct from generic interpretation, as discussed in (Mathew and Katz, 2009). But, being proxies, our features in this domain can only give us probable inferences. Whatever system that is built on them needs to provide for means to override them.

[4]Beaver goes on discussion some factors that might play a role in spoken language and points to an information structure based solution. The ingredients of that solution will not be computationally available for some time to come.

Acknowledgments

Thanks to Cleo Condoravdi and Stanley Peters for comments and discussions and to Marianne Naval and Miriam Connor for running the experiment.

The authors gratefully acknowledge the support of Defense Advanced Research Projects Agency (DARPA) Machine Reading Program under Air Force Research Laboratory (AFRL) prime contract no. FA8750-09-C-0181. Any opinions, findings, and conclusions or recommendations expressed in this material are those of the authors and do not necessarily reflect the view of DARPA, AFRL, or the US government.

References

David Beaver. 2010. Have you noticed that you belly button lint colour is related to the colour of your clothing? In R. Bauerle, U. Reyle, and T. E. Zimmermann, editors, *Presuppositions and Discourse: Essays offered to Hans Kamp*, pages 65–99. Elsevier.

Lauri Karttunen. 1971. Implicative verbs. *Language*, 47:340–358.

Lauri Karttunen. 1974. Presupposition and linguistic context. *Theoretical Linguistics*, 1(1):181–194.

Lauri Karttunen. 2012. Simple and phrasal implicatives. In **SEM 2012*, pages 124–131, Montréal, Canada. Association for Computational Linguistics.

Lauri Karttunen. 2013. You will be lucky to break even. In Tracy Holloway King and Valeria dePaiva, editors, *From Quirky Case to Representing Space: Papers in Honor of Annie Zaenen*, pages 167–180. CSLI Publications, Stanford, CA.

Paul Kiparsky and Carol Kiparsky. 1970. Fact. In M. Bierwisch and K. E. Heidolph, editors, *Progress in Linguistics*, pages 143–173. Mouton, Hague.

Karin Kipper-Schuler. 2005. *Verbnet: a broad-coverage comprehensive verb lexicon*. Ph.D. thesis, University of Pennsylvania.

Angelika Kratzer. 2012. *Modals and Conditionals. New and Revised Perspectives*. Oxford University Press, Oxford, U.K.

Terence Langendoen and Harris Savin. 1971. The projection problem for presuppositions. In C.J. Fillmore and D.T. Langendoen, editors, *Studies in Linguistic Semantics*. Holt, Rinehart and Winston, New York.

Bill MacCartney and Christopher D. Manning. 2009. An extended model of natural logic. In *Proceedings IWCS-8 '09 Proceedings of the Eighth International Conference on Computational Semantics*, pages 140–156. University of Tilburg.

Thomas A. Mathew and E. Graham Katz. 2009. Supervised categorization for habitual versus episodic sentences. In *The Sixth Midwest Computational Linguistics Colloquium 2009 at Indiana University Bloomington*.

Rowan Nairn, Cleo Condoravdi, and Lauri Karttunen. 2006. Computing relative polarity for textual inference. In *ICoS-5*, pages 67–76.

Neal R. Norrick. 1978. *Factive Adjectives and the Theory of Factivity*. Niemeyer.

F. R. Palmer. 2001. *Mood and Modality*. Cambridge University Press, Cambridge, U.K.

Christopher Potts. 2005. *The Logic of Conventional Implicatures*. Cambridge University Press, Cambridge, United Kingdom.

Roser Saurí and James Pustejovsky. 2009. Factbank 1.0. Linguistic Data Consortium, September.

Roser Saurí and James Pustejovsky. 2012. Are you sure that this happened? assessing the factuality degree of events in text. *Computational Linguistics*, 38(2):261–299.

Roser Saurí. 2008. *A Factuality Profiler for Eventualities in Text*. Ph.D. thesis, Brandeis University.

More Than Only Noun-Noun Compounds: Towards an Annotation Scheme for the Semantic Modelling of Other Noun Compound Types

Ben Verhoeven
CLiPS - Computational Linguistics Group
University of Antwerp
Antwerp, Belgium
ben.verhoeven@ua.ac.be

Gerhard B. van Huyssteen
Centre for Text Technology (CTexT)
North-West University
Potchefstroom, South Africa
gerhard.vanhuyssteen@nwu.ac.za

Abstract

The computational processing of compound semantics poses several interesting challenges. Up to now, the processing of nominal compounds with non-noun left-hand constituents (henceforth XN compounds) has not received any attention, despite the fact that these also seem to be rather productive in Germanic languages. In our research project, we aim to fill this hiatus by investigating various kinds of compounds in Afrikaans and Dutch, develop annotation protocols and data sets, and model the semantics of such compounds. In this publication we present the alpha version of an annotation protocol that was designed for both descriptive linguistic and computational linguistic purposes. We describe the protocol development and discuss the current version.

1 Introduction

Within the field of natural language understanding, the semantic processing of compounds poses several interesting challenges, including issues related to compositionality, ambiguity, and contextual interpretation (see Girju *et al.* (2005) for a more elaborate discussion). The majority of research up to now has focused on English, but surprisingly, virtually no research has been done for other (Germanic) languages (cf. Verhoeven, 2012; Verhoeven, Daelemans & van Huyssteen, 2012). Also, given that noun-noun (NN) compounds are by far the most productive form of compounding in English (Plag, 2003: 145), it is to be expected that research on the semantic analysis of English compounds (both in descriptive linguistics and computational linguistics) has thus far focused almost exclusively on NN compounds (see Ó Séaghdha (2008) for a comprehensive overview, as well as Adams (2001: 83ff) for a synopsis). A computational understanding of compound semantics is of importance for commercial applications such as machine translation systems, where one often has to paraphrase compounds (i.e. make the compound semantics explicit at surface level) to be able to translate them into languages that are not as productive in compounding, or that has different compound constructions (Nakov, 2008).

Second to NN compounds, nominal compounds with non-noun left-hand constituents (henceforth XN compounds; i.e. other nominal compound types) seems to be the most productive in English (see Lieber, 2009), and probably in other Germanic languages as well. However, as far as we could establish, no research has been done on the computational modelling of the semantics of XN compounds in any language; hence, no annotation guidelines, data sets or prior experiments are available. In our research project, we aim to fill this hiatus by investigating various kinds of compounds in Afrikaans and Dutch, develop annotation protocols and data sets, and model the semantics of such compounds.

In this contribution, we present a first version of an annotation protocol for XN nouns, specifically for Afrikaans and Dutch (but also referring to English in passing). The next section presents a brief linguistic description of XN compounding in Afrikaans and Dutch. In section 3 we discuss some general principles for compound annotation, before presenting the detailed protocol. In section 4 we

	Afrikaans (Afr.)	Dutch (Du.)	English (Eng.)
NN	*tafelblad* 'table top'	*pannenkoek* 'pancake'	*car key*
VN[1]	*faksmasjien* 'fax machine'	*leesbril* 'reading glasses'	*skateboard*
AN[2]	*geelwortel* 'carrot'	*geelzucht* 'yellow fever; jaundice'	*lightweight*
PN[3]	*onderrok* 'under skirt; petticoat'	*achterlicht* 'back light'	*undertone*
QN[4]	*agthoek* 'octagon'	*eenoog* 'cyclops	*twoface*

Table 1: Examples of NN and XN compounds in Afrikaans, Dutch and English.

conclude with a view on future research.

2 XN Compounding in Germanic Languages

Compounding is a highly productive word-formation process in most languages (Plag, 2003), and as such has received much attention in research literature (e.g. Lieber and Štekauer, 2009). With regard to typologies of compounding, Scalise and Bisetto (2009) provide a comprehensive overview, and also present the most recent morphological compound classification scheme that is based on the compound's internal syntactic function. With regard to the syntactic form of compounds, Plag (2003) indicates that nominal compounds occur widely in English (with NN compounds the most common type); Don (2009: 370-371) maintains the same for Dutch: "Nominal compounds are by far the most productive type, although other types (adjectival and verbal) exist and can also be formed productively". Since the same holds true for German (Neef, 2009: 388) and Danish (Bauer, 2009: 404), we may safely assume that it also applies to Afrikaans, a West Germanic language, closely related to Dutch. Compare Table 1 for examples of NN and XN compounds in Afrikaans, Dutch and English.

The most important challenge with regard to interpreting VN compounds is whether the V should be interpreted as a V or an N in languages where a distinction between these forms are not marked overtly, or where the (lack of) morphology could lead to ambiguous interpretations. For example, in *swimming pool*, the question is whether *swimming* should be interpreted as a V ('pool where one swims') or as a N ('pool for the act of swimming') (see Lieber, 2009: 361). When using the continuous participle form of English verbs (the *-ing* forms) as a noun, it "does not describe a single episode of the process, but instead rather refers to it in a generalised, even generic fashion" (Langacker, 1987: 208). It is therefore natural to assign an N interpretation to *swimming*, and consequently regard *swimming pool* (and the likes) as an NN compound.

In contrast, in the Dutch *zwembad* **swim+bath** 'swimming pool', a V interpretation is assigned to the first constituent (a verbal stem), i.e. 'bath where one swims'. Most of the time, a verbal interpretation is the only option, since the infinitive form of the verb (e.g. *zwemmen*) is usually used as the nominalised form (as in *Ik hou van zwemmen* **I like of swim-INF** 'I like swimming'). Hence, in Dutch we often find VN compounds.

Since Afrikaans does not have an overtly marked infinitive form of the verb, it might seem to be more ambiguous to distinguish whether *swem* in *swembad* **swim+bath** 'swimming pool' is a verb or a noun (i.e. the part-of-speech category of *swem* remains ambiguous). However, because of the close relationship between Dutch and Afrikaans, we will treat their compounds equally and thus consider these stems as verbs; see Section 3.1. below.

With regard to AN compounds, we should note that none of the three Germanic languages under discussion allow for productive AN compounding, since an A and N usually forms a noun phrase (NP), e.g. *white cloud* is considered an NP, and not an AN compound. However, all three languages do allow for compounding when there are signs of extension of meaning. For example, a *blackboard* is more than just 'a board with the colour black' - it is more specifically 'a dark-coloured surface where one could write on with chalk'. In all three lan-

[1]VN = Verb-Noun Compound
[2]AN = Adjective/Adverb-Noun Compound
[3]PN = Preposition-Noun Compound
[4]QN = Quantifier/Numeral-Noun Compound

guages, such cases are most often written as one word, and thus more easily distinguishable from NPs. (Of course, the orthography is a result of the compounding process, rather than a cause.) Note that it seems as if this phenomenon is found more frequently in Afrikaans orthography than in English or Dutch, e.g. Afr. *witwyn*, Du. *witte wijn*, Eng. *white wine*; or Afr. *swartmark*, Du. *zwarte markt*, Eng. *black market* 'underground economy for trading illegal goods'; further comparative linguistic research is needed to confirm this observation. All cases of AN compounds should therefore be considered lexicalised, although certain patterns in the semantics of such compounds might become apparent (see Section 3.2 below).

Similarly, all QN compounds in these three languages are lexicalised - see Afr. *agthoek*, Du. *eenoog*, Eng. *twoface* in Table 1 above. However, a special case of phrasal compound could be distinguished: $[[\mathrm{Q\ N}]_{NP}\ \mathrm{N}]_{\mathrm{N}}$, as in Afr. *derdejaarstudent*, Du. *tweepersoonsbed*, Eng. *three-phase electricity*. Booij (2002: 150-151) presents an argument that one could consider such constructions also as NN compounds (i.e. $[[\mathrm{QN}]_{\mathrm{N}}\ \mathrm{N}]_{\mathrm{N}}$), but we are of contention that it makes more sense in the context of compound semantics to consider it phrasal compounds, i.e. a *derdejaarstudent* is 'a student in his/her third year', a *tweepersoonsbed* is 'a bed for two people', and *three-phase electricity* is 'electricity with three phases'. Currently, such compounds are excluded from our focus, since this protocol only deals with two-part compounds, as will be indicated in the next section.

3 Protocol Design

The design of our XN compound semantics protocol is based on the work by Ó Séaghdha (2008) on NN compounds. We adopted his approach of semantic categorisation and used his categories as basis for the construction of a protocol for XN compounds in Dutch and Afrikaans. The protocol deals mainly with two-part compounds, and hence phrasal compounds and recursive compounds are excluded from the scope of our current research.

Also note that the version of the protocol presented here is still an alpha version, and has not yet been verified (i.e. tested and extended) on a representative dataset of compounds. A complete version of this protocol, as well as subsequent updated versions of the protocol are available on the Sourceforge page of the AuCoPro project[5].

In concordance with the approach of Verhoeven (2012) and Verhoeven, Daelemans and Van Huyssteen (2012) on the computational understanding of compounds, all compounds that are listed in a standard explanatory dictionary are considered lexicalised when using the protocol for computational experiments. These lexicalised words do not need a computational interpretation, because their meanings are already present in the dictionary glosses. For purposes of descriptive linguistics, using dictionary compounds in non-lexicalised categories is allowed when their meanings are the product of a clear relation between the two constituents. This distinction between lexicalised and non-lexicalised leaves room for interpretation in descriptive linguistics, but it is a practical measure for computational purposes.

Exocentric compounds, such as Afr. *banggat* **afraid+bottom** 'person that is easily frightened'; Du. *kaalkop* **bald+head** 'person with a bald head', Eng. *uphill* (i.e. $[\mathrm{PN}]_{Adv}$) are always lexicalised and thus also tagged as lexicalised, following the LEX category of Ó Séaghdha (2008). Endocentric compounds can be either lexicalised or non-lexicalised (and thus productive). Endocentric compounds with lexicalised meanings do not explicate the relation between the constituents in a predictable manner, i.e. they are fully non-compositional. There is thus one more differentiation within the lexicalised category: such compounds can be classified as either endocentric or exocentric.

The main distinction between compound types in our protocol is between the parts-of-speech of the first constituent. We consider the following main categories: verb, adjective (or adverb), quantifier (or numeral), or preposition.

3.1 Verb-Noun Compounds (VN)

This category contains two-part compounds that take a verb as a first constituent and a noun as a second constituent. The first constituent will only be considered a verb if it cannot be interpreted as a noun. That is, in *zwembad* **swim+pool** 'swimming

[5]https://sourceforge.net/projects/aucopro/

pool', the constituent *zwem* can only be interpreted as a verb, and is hence assigned a V interpretation (unlike the case in English; see discussion above).

3.1.1. Event

This category is based on the INST and ACTOR categories in Ó Séaghdha's protocol (2008). In our protocol, the verb describes an action in which the noun is some sort of participant. There are three subcategories to this rule: the nominal element can be the subject, object or instrument of the action described by the verb. Although it might be interesting to consider using semantic roles (e.g. from Frame Semantics) as subcategories, this might also lead to an abundance of fine-grained semantic classes, resulting in more problems than gains for automatic classification. We opine that such a classification task (i.e. using fine-grained semantic roles) would be a particularly hard task even for human annotators, while the semantic role information could be deduced broadly from the combination of the verb semantics with the syntactic role of the noun.

- Subject
  ('N that Vs; the goal of N is to V')
  Afr. *snydokter* **cut+doctor** 'doctor that cuts; surgeon'
  Du. *gloeilamp* **glow+lamp** 'lamp that glows; lightbulb'

- Object
  ('N that is (being) V-ed; VN is the result of V-INF; the goal of N is to be V-ed')
  Afr. *snyblomme* **cut+flowers** 'the goal of the flowers is to be cut'
  Du. *werpbal* **throw+ball** 'ball that is thrown'

- Instrument
  ('N is used to V-INF')
  Afr. *kapbyl* **chop+axe** 'axe used to chop down trees'
  Du. *leesbril* **read+glasses** 'glasses that are used to read; reading glasses'

3.1.2. Location

This category practically equals Ó Séaghdha's IN category (2008). It contains those VN compounds in which the noun is a spatial or temporal location (two subcategories) of the action described by the verb.

- Space
  ('V in (neighbourhood of) N; N where one Vs')
  Afr. *herstelsentrum* **recover+centre** 'centre where people recover from injuries or operations'
  Du. *slaapkamer* **sleep+room** 'room where one sleeps; bed room'

- Time
  ('N during which one Vs')
  Afr. *bakleifase* **quarrel+fase** 'fase during which one quarrels'
  Du. *regeerperiode* **rule+period** 'period during which someone rules'

3.1.3 Composed of

This category can best be compared with the part-whole and group interpretation of the HAVE category in Ó Séaghdha (2008). The noun is some sort of collection of the action described by the verb. The compound can best be paraphrased as 'N consists of V', e.g.:

> Afr. *skokterapie* **shock+therapy** 'therapy that consists of shocking the patient'
> Du. *niesbui* **sneeze+shower** 'rapid succession of sneezes'

3.1.4. Lexicalised

As indicated above, lexicalised compounds can be either endocentric or exocentric; both subcategories are excluded from computational experiments.

- Endocentric
  Afr. *snyhou* **cut+stroke** 'kind of tennis stroke'
  Du. *draaibal* **turn+ball** 'ball that is kicked with a turning effect'

- Exocentric
  Afr. *speeltuin* **play+garden** 'playground'
  Du. *verzamelwoede* **collect+anger** 'urge or mania to collect things'

3.2 Adjective-Noun Compounds (AN)

In our research thus far, we found all AN compounds to be lexicalised, since the normal pattern in Germanic languages is to consider A + N as a syntactic phrase (see Section 2 above). We will therefore not consider this category for computational experiments, but for descriptive completeness, we do posit some subcategories for concatenated AN compounds.

3.2.1. Lexicalised

- Endocentric

Most examples under this category can be matched to certain aspects of Ó Séaghdhas (2008) ABOUT category, where the first constituent (A) describes a characteristic of the concept defined by the second constituent (N). Note that the A provides a more precise, fuller specification of the concept in the domain of instantiation (Langacker, 2008: 134-136), invoking a variety of cognitive domains (Langacker, 1987: 117). From our initial data analyses, we posit "Duration" and "Colour" as prototypical domains (specifically for Afrikaans), but we also posit an "Other" category, leaving the door open that more subcategories could be defined in further linguistic research and data analysis.

- Duration
('kind of N that is A')
Afr. *langverlof* **long+leave** 'kind of leave that is longer than what is normally taken'
Du. no examples found

- Colour
('kind of N that is A')
Afr. *geelrys* **yellow+rice** 'kind of rice that is yellow'
Du. *rodekool* **red+cabbage** 'kind of cabbage that is red'

- Other qualities
('kind of N that has the quality expressed by A')
Afr. *sterkstroom* **strong+current** 'high voltage; the power current is strong'
Du. *hogeschool* **high+school** 'school for higher education'

- Exocentric

This category of lexicalised AN compounds contains those compounds of which the semantic head is not present in the compound. Often, they are possessive compounds where the compound is an entity that has the characteristic described by the noun modified by the adjective.

- Attributive (Scalise and Bisetto, 2009: 36); also known as possessive or bahuvrihi compounds (Bauer, 2004: 21)
Afr. *luigat* **lazy+bottom** 'person that is lazy'
Du. *kaalkop* **bald+head** 'person that has a bald head'

- Other
Afr. *groenskrif* **green+script** 'first draft of legislation; green paper'
Du. *blijspel* **happy+game** 'theatre play that is supposed to amuse people'

3.3 Quantifier-Noun Compounds (QN)

In this category, we consider quantifiers and numerals as first constituent of a two-part compound that has a noun as a second constituent.

3.3.1. Quantity-Object

The quantifier that specifies the quantity of N within a larger phrasal compound (i.e. $[\,[Q{+}N]_{NP}\ N]_{N}$) is the only productive form of QN compounding (e.g. Afr. *sewejaardroogte* **seven+year+drought** 'seven-year drought') (see Section 2 above). Since these are not two-part compounds, they fall outside the scope of our current research project.

3.3.2. Lexicalised

Many of the lexicalised QN compounds are exocentric compounds, with a notable number of them being plant and animal names.

- Endocentric
No examples in Afrikaans or Dutch have been found yet.

- Exocentric - Attributive
(compound is 'entity that has Q number of N')
Afr. *vierkleur* **four+colour** 'flag of the old Transvaal Republic'
Du. *duizendpoot* **thousand+leg** 'centipede'.

3.4 Preposition-Noun Compounds (PN)

All compounds that have a preposition as a first constituent and a noun as the second constituent belong in this class, even when the prepositions have adopted a more abstract or metaphorical meaning.

3.4.1. Location

This category also relates to Ó Séaghdha's IN category (2008). The concept described by N is at a position P of an undefined other concept. In three different subclasses, the preposition describes a spatial, temporal, or more abstract/metaphorical position. The paraphrases of these categories contain an undefined concept 'G' that is used as reference point (i.e. grounding point).

- Space
  ('N is spatially at position P relative to G')
  Afr. *onderrok* **under+skirt** 'skirt worn under other skirt'
  Du. *achterlicht* **behind+light** 'light at behind of car or bike; rear light'

- Time
  ('N is temporally at position P relative to G')
  Afr. *voormiddag* **before+noon** 'forenoon'
  Du. *nagesprek* **after+talk** 'conversation after previous event'

- Abstract/Metaphorical
  ('N is at abstract position P relative to G')
  Afr. *byverdienste* **by+income** 'additional income to normal income'
  Du. *overgewicht* **over+weight** 'the weight that is over the normal'

3.4.2. Process-based

We assume this kind of PN compound to be related to some kind of process. The noun goes in the direction described by the preposition ('N goes in direction P'), e.g.:

Afr. *opmars* **up+march** 'march'
Du. *overstap* **over+step** 'transfer on public transport'

3.4.3. Lexicalised

- Endocentric
  Afr. *optog* **up+trip** 'procession'
  Du. *uitgroeisel* **out+growth** 'excrescence'

- Exocentric
  Afr. *insig* **in+sight** 'insight'
  Du. *nageboorte* **after+birth** 'afterbirth'

4 Conclusion and Future Work

We have presented the alpha version of an annotation protocol for the semantics of Dutch and Afrikaans noun compounds which have a non-noun as a first constituent. Although this protocol is primarily designed for computational linguistic purposes, we have also indicated some categories relevant to (comparative) descriptive linguistics. Basic points of departure (based on work by Ó Séaghdha (2008)) have also been described.

During the development of the protocol, we came across some interesting findings that should be verified in further research. For example, it seems as if all two-part AN and QN compounds are lexicalised, probably because the more regular A + N and Q + N constructions in Germanic languages are syntactic phrases. In some categories we could not find examples yet, these should be investigated in further corpus-based/-driven research.

Also, the way we constructed the event-based category for VN compounds (see Section 3.1.1. above) is open for closer scrutiny. Having separate subcategories for subject, object, instrument and goal/result relations seems an interesting adaptation of the INST and ACTOR categories in Ó Séaghdha (2008). We believe it is worth considering the adjustment of Ó Séaghdha's INST and ACTOR categories to be more like our categories in combining the several participants of the event on which the compound is based. This would, in our opinion, make the annotation process easier because it does away with the 'direction' of the annotation rules that Ó Séaghdha uses.

As part of the continuous development of our current protocol, we are currently in the process of annotating Dutch and Afrikaans compounds, using this protocol. The annotation process will proceed as described by Verhoeven (2012). We are using the compound database CKarma (CTexT, 2005) for Afrikaans and a compound list extracted from the e-Lex corpus for Dutch[6]. Eventually, this annotated data will be used in computational experiments to predict the semantics of a variety of compounds in these two languages. The results of these experiments will be published later.

[6]This list was extracted from the e-Lex corpus and annotated by Lieve Macken from LT3 at Ghent University College.

Future work on the semantics of compounds includes, but is not limited to: the investigation of affixoid-noun compounds where an adverb-like affixoid combines with a noun, such as Afr. *laatherfs* **late+autumn** 'late autumn'; Du. *tegenaanval* **against+attack** 'counter-attack'; and Eng. *co-inhabitant*; investigation of the semantics of compounds with different parts-of-speech such as XA (e.g. Afr. *bloedrooi* **blood+red** 'very red') and XV (e.g. Afr. *stofsuig* **dust+suck** 'vacuum/hoover') compounds; research into regularities that could be found in the construction and meaning of phrasal compounds.

Acknowledgments

Automatic Compound Processing (AuCoPro[7]) is a collaborative project by research groups of the North-West University (Potchefstroom, South Africa), the University of Antwerp (Belgium) and Tilburg University (The Netherlands), and is funded through a research grant from the Nederlandse Taalunie (Dutch Language Union) and the South African Department of Arts and Culture (DAC), as well as a grant of the South African National Research Foundation (NRF) (grant number 81794).

We would like to acknowledge the work of Joanie Liversage (North-West University), who attempted a first analysis of XN compounds in her third-year mini-dissertation, as well as the inputs of Walter Daelemans (University of Antwerp).

References

Valerie Adams. 2001. *Complex Words in English*. Longman, Harlow, UK.

Laurie Bauer. 2004. *A Glossary of Morphology*. Edinburgh University Press, Edinburgh, UK.

Laurie Bauer. 2009. IE, Germanic: Danish. In Rochelle Lieber and Pavol Štekauer, editors, *The Oxford Handbook of Compounding*, pages 400–416. Oxford University Press, Oxford, UK.

Geert Booij. 2002. *The Morphology of Dutch*. Oxford University Press, Oxford, UK.

CTexT. 2005. CKarma (C5 KompositumAnaliseerder vir Robuuste Morfologiese Analise). [C5 Compound Analyser for Robust Morphological Analysis]. Centre for Text Technology (CTexT), North-West University, Potchefstroom, South Africa.

Jan Don. 2009. IE, Germanic: Dutch. In Rochelle Lieber and Pavol Štekauer, editors, *The Oxford Handbook of Compounding*, pages 370–385. Oxford University Press, Oxford, UK.

Roxana Girju, Dan Moldovan, Marta Tatu, and Daniel Antohe. 2005. On the semantics of noun compounds. *Computer Speech and Language*, 19:479–496.

Ronald Langacker. 1987. *Foundations of Cognitive Grammar: Volume 1 - Theoretical Prerequisites*. Stanford University Press, Stanford.

Rochelle Lieber and Pavol Štekauer. 2009. Introduction: status and definition of compounding. In Rochelle Lieber and Pavol Štekauer, editors, *The Oxford Handbook of Compounding*, pages 3–18. Oxford University Press, Oxford, UK.

Rochelle Lieber. 2009. IE, Germanic: English. In Rochelle Lieber and Pavol Štekauer, editors, *The Oxford Handbook of Compounding*, pages 357–369. Oxford University Press, Oxford, UK.

Preslav Nakov. 2008. Noun compound interpretation using paraphrasing verbs: Feasibility study. In *Proceedings of the 13th International Conference on Artificial Intelligence: Methodology, Systems, Applications (AIMSA08)*.

Martin Neef. 2009. IE, Germanic: German. In Rochelle Lieber and Pavol Štekauer, editors, *The Oxford Handbook of Compounding*, pages 386–399. Oxford University Press, Oxford, UK.

Diarmuid Ó Séaghdha. 2008. *Learning compound noun semantics*. Ph.D. thesis, University of Cambridge, Cambridge, UK.

Ingo Plag. 2003. *Word-Formation in English*. Cambridge University Press, Cambridge, UK.

Sergio Scalise and Antonietta Bisetto. 2009. The classification of compounds. In Rochelle Lieber and Pavol Štekauer, editors, *The Oxford Handbook of Compounding*, pages 34–53. Oxford University Press, Oxford, UK.

Ben Verhoeven, Walter Daelemans, and Gerhard B. van Huyssteen. 2012. Classification of noun-noun compound semantics in Dutch and Afrikaans. In *Proceedings of the Twenty-Third Annual Symposium of the Pattern Recognition Association of South Africa (PRASA 2012)*, pages 121–125, Pretoria, South Africa.

Ben Verhoeven. 2012. A computational semantic analysis of noun compounds in Dutch. Master's thesis, University of Antwerp, Antwerp, Belgium.

[7] http://tinyurl.com/aucopro

Issues in the addition of ISO standard annotations to the Switchboard corpus

Harry Bunt
TiCC, Tilburg Center for Cognition and Communication
Tilburg University
Tilburg, The N etherlands
harry.bunt@uvt.nl

Alex C. Fang and Xiaoyue Liu
City University of Hong Kong
Department of Chinese, Translation, and Linguistics
Hong Kong SAR
a.c.fang@cityu.edu.hk
xyliu@cityu.edu.hk

Jing Cao
College of Foreign Languages
Zhongnan University of Economics and Law
Wuhan, China
c_jinhk@yahoo.cn

Volha Petukhova
Department of Spoken Language Systems
Saarland University
Saarbrücken, Germany
v.petukhova@lsv.uni-saarland.de

Abstract

This paper analyzes the issues that arise when trying to add annotations to the dialogues in the Switchboard corpus according to ISO standard 24617-2, exploiting the existing SWBD-DAMSL annotations. These issues relate to differences between the two tag sets; to the highly multidimensional view that underlies the ISO standard; to differences in segmenting the dialogues into functional units; to the use of in-line markups for certain phenomena in Switchboard, and to the use of intra-dialogue dependence relations as defined in the ISO standard.

The analysis is supplemented by a discussion of how the existing annotations may be helpful to semi-automatically create a fully-fledged ISO standard annotation alongside the existing SWBD-DAMSL annotation.

1 Introduction

In September 2013 the International Organisation for Standardisation ISO published the international standard 24617-2[1], a comprehensive application-independent scheme for dialogue act annotation that is both empirically and theoretically well-founded, that can deal with typed, spoken, and multimodal dialogue, and that can be used effectively by human annotators and by automatic annotation methods.

With the aim of building a large corpus of dialogues, annotated according to this standard, an effort was initiated to create ISO 24617-2 annotations for the dialogues in the Switchboard corpus, which forms a valuable resource for the study of spoken dialogue.[2] In particular, this effort exploits the similarities between the ISO 24617-2 and the SWBD-DAMSL scheme (Jurafsky et al., 1997) by semi-automatically converting SWBD-DAMSL annotations into ISO 24617-2 annotations where possible. An additional benefit of this approach is that it allows an in-depth comparison between the two annotation schemes.

Fang et al. (2011) have described initial explorations in this project, and Fang et al. (2012) have described the possibilities and limitations of automatically converting SWBD-DAMSL tags to ISO 24617-2 tags. This paper deals with other issues, relating in particular to (1) the highly multidimensional approach to annotation that underlies the ISO standard more clearly than the annotations in the Switchboard corpus; (2) the segmentation of the Switchboard dialogues into 'slash-units' rather than into 'functional segments', as the ISO standard requires; (3) the use of certain in-line markups and tagging of non-functional phenomena in the Switchboard dialogues; and (4) the annotation of dependence relations between units in a dialogue according to the ISO standard.

Example (1), showing a small dialogue fragment (from Switchboard dialogue sw01-0105), as marked up in the Switchboard corpus and as annotated according to ISO 24617-2, illustrates some of the differences between the two approaches.

(1) a. (dialogue sw01-0105 lines 0007-0008)
A003: `qw^d` {D So } when you say the morning news, or evening news or national news is when? /
B004: `sd` {F Uh, } evening news at six thirty I believe /

b. ISO-24617-2 segmentation:
fs1 = So
fs2 = when you say the morning news, or evening news, or national news, is when?

[1] See the official description of the standard in ISO 24617-2:2013, and summary descriptions in Bunt et al. (2010; 2012).

[2] The Switchboard Dialogue Act Corpus is distributed by LDC.

fs3 = Uh

fs4 = evening news is at six thirty I believe /

c. ISO 24617-2 annotation:

```
<diaml xmlns:
 "http://www.iso.org/diaml/"/>
<dialogueAct xml:id="a1"
 target="#fs1"
 sender="#a" addressee="#b"
 communicativeFunction=
   "turnTake"
 dimension="turnManagement"/>
<dialogueAct xml:id="a2"
 target="#fs1"
 sender="#a" addressee="#b"
 communicativeFunction=
   "stalling"
 dimension="timeManagement"/>
<dialogueAct xml:id="a3"
 target="#fs2"
 sender="#a" addressee="#b"
 communicativeFunction=
   "propositionalQuestion"
 dimension="task"/>
<dialogueAct xml:id="a4"
 target="#fs3"
 sender="#b" addressee="#a"
 communicativeFunction=
   "stalling"
 dimension="timeManagement"/>
<dialogueAct xml:id="a5"
 target="#fs3"
 sender="#b" addressee="#a"
 comm.Function="turnTake"
 dimension="turnManagement"/>
 <dialogueAct xml:id="a6"
 target="#fs4"
 sender="#b" addressee="#a"
 communicativeFunction=
   "answer"
 certainty="uncertain"
 dimension="task"
 functionalDependence="#a3"/>
</diaml>
```

SWBD-DAMSL annotations and ISO 24617-2 annotations clearly use very different representation formats. SWBD-DAMSL makes use of functional tags like `qw^d` (which stands for "Declarative Wh-Question") and `sd` (for "Statement non-opinion"), in the form of strings attached to stretches of text delineated by "/", so-called "slash-units" (see Section 2.1). Other information is encoded as in-line markups, such as in (1a) a discourse marker by '{D So }' and a filled pause by '{F Uh }'; and the identity of the speaker is encoded in line numbers like 'A003' and 'B004'.

ISO standard annotations represent all the information in the form of XML-expressions, making use of the XML-based annotation language DiAML (Dialogue Act Markup Language) which is defined as part of the standard. These annotations are in stand-off form, with an attribute `@target` whose value identifies the stretch of dialogue that the annotation applies to (a 'functional segment', see Section 2.1). The annotations in DiAML include not only an identification of the speaker, as in Switchboard, but also of one or more addressees (the attribute `@addressee` may have multiple values); a specification not only of the communicative function of a dialogue act expressed by the functional segment but also of the communicative dimension that the act belongs to (such as the task that motivates the dialogue, the dimension of turn-taking, or the dimension of time management)[3]; and an indication of relations among dialogue acts, in this example an indication of the question that is answered by an Answer act.

An analysis of the similarities and differences between the SWBD-DAMSL and ISO 24617-2 tag sets in Fang et al. (2011; 2012) shows that 14 of the SWBD-DAMSL tags exactly match an ISO 24617-2 communicative function tag, and 27 SWBD-DAMSL tags correspond to 9 ISO standard tags. The latter is due to the fact that SWBD-DAMSL sometimes makes distinctions which are not motivated semantically but syntactically or lexically; for example, the tags Yes-answer, Affirmative non-yes answer, No-answer, and Negative non-no answer all correspond to the single ISO tag Answer. In the case of exact matches and many-to-one matches, the conversion from SWBD-DAMSL tags to ISO communicative function tags can be done automatically; Fang et al. (2012) report that this can be done for 187,768 of the 223,606 units annotated in the Switchboard corpus, which amounts to 84,0% of the corpus.

Replacing SWBD-DAMSL tags by ISO communicative function tags does not create full ISO standard annotations, however, as example (1) showed; not only do we have to replace the tags `qw^d` and `sd` by the appropriate ISO tags (Set-Question and Inform, respectively) but we also have to consider (1) for each communicative

[3]The ISO standard distinguishes nine dimensions: Task, Turn Management, Time Management, Auto-Feedback, Allo-Feedback, Own Communication Management, Partner Communication Management, Discourse Structuring, and Social Obligations Management. For definitions see Bunt (2009).

function the dimension in which it is used; (2) the addition of communicative functions in those dimensions where SWBD-DAMSL doesn't have any, such as turn management; (3) what to do with the in-line markup of discourse connectives like and filled pauses; (4) how to produce the ISO qualifiers, like `certainty="uncertain"` and relations between dialogue acts, like `functionalDependence="#a3"`.

This paper is structured as follows. Section 2 discusses issues relating to the segmentation of dialogues into meaningful units. Section 3 discusses the annotation of in-line markups. Section 4 discusses the treatment of some phenomena that are not annotated in Switchboard. The concluding Section 6 summarizes the analysis of the main issues involved in adding ISO standard annotations to the Switchboard corpus, and indicates for each of these issues how the additions could be made, exploiting the existing SWBD-DAMSL annotations and the in-line markups of various phenomena.

2 Segmentation

2.1 Slash units versus functional segments

The annotations in the Switchboard corpus make use of a segmentation of dialogues into so-called 'slash units', defined by Meteer & Taylor (1995), as *"Maximally a sentence, but possibly a smaller unit. Intuitively, slash-units below the sentence level correspond to those parts of the narrative which are not sentential but which the annotator interprets as complete"*. Slash units are allowed to span (parts of) multiple turns by the same speaker, separated by a contribution from another speaker, and in that sense to be discontinuous, as in the following example (from Core & Allen, 1997):

	u:	<u>take the product to</u>
(2)	s:	yes?
	u:	<u>to Corning</u>

The Switchboard segmentation follows the strategy for dialogue annotation with DAMSL tags described by Core and Allen (1997), who call these units 'utterances'. Utterances are allowed to be discontinuous only in case of an interruption by another speaker, as in (2), and are not allowed to overlap with other units. Disfluencies such as hesitations (like *uh* or *um*), and restarts like *I mean*, are thus not treated as units with a communicative function. With reference to the repair in example (3), Core and Allen (1997) note that they do not view *Tuesday I mean Friday* as a functional unit, since that *"would mean cutting off "Friday" from "we'll go Tuesday". DAMSL is not designed for annotating speech repairs, reference, or other intra-clause relations so we decided to use a simple definition of an utterance that leaves out such phenomena"*.

(3) we'll go Tuesday I mean Friday

This strategy is clearly inadequate for annotating phenomena of own communication management and time management. ISO 24617-2 supports the annotation of communicative functions in these dimensions, in view of the frequent occurrence of stallings and self-corrections in spontaneous speech, and takes over the approach to segmentation developed for dialogue analysis using the DIT^{++} annotation scheme (Bunt, 2009). This approach defines a *functional unit* as a minimal stretch of communicative behaviour that has a communicative function (and possibly more than one function) (Geertzen et al., 2007). Utterance (3) would be segmented as shown in (4), where the parts in boldface form the discontinuous segment *we'll go Friday*, expressing an inform act, and the underlined part *Tuesday I mean Friday* forms an overlapping functional segment that expresses a self-correction.

(4) **we'll go** <u>*Tuesday I mean* **Friday**</u>

A disadvantage of treating an entire utterance like (3) as a single unit, is that any self-correction which it contains is associated with the entire utterance, which is not accurate. This causes a serious problem when a slash unit contains more than one stalling or self-correction, since the annotation cannot distinguish between these. For example, in (5) (from Switchboard dialogue sw00-0004, line 30) a stalling is expressed by the filled pauses `{F uh, }` `{F uh, }` and another one by the repetition `[ to the, + to the]`.

(5) you wouldn't have this {F uh, } {F uh, } theatrics where the lawyer jumps up and presents it [to the, + to the] jury /

Some 25-30% of the slash units in the Switchboard corpus contain a stalling or a self-correction, and an estimated 6% more than one of these, so the inability to correctly annotate these is a serious limitation. The in-line markup indicates each filled pause, but does not assign an interpretation to it. The annotation of disfluencies is discussed further in Section 3.

2.2 Mono- versus multifunctionality

The annotations in the Switchboard corpus are monofunctional, in the sense that only one SWBD-DAMSL tag is assigned to each slash unit. There are only a few cases in the corpus where more than one tag has been asigned; see the examples in (6):

(6) a. (dialogue sw07-0701 line 0161-B108-03) B: school's very important I'm an educator myself and my wife teaches/

b. (dialogue sw07-0701 line 0083-B060-05) B: {C but } I think that if you did something, for example, to an individual and caused them to lose the ability to earn a living, I remember a man drove by randomly shot a woman in the head while she was driving –

c. (dialogue sw07-0701 line 0716-A107-01) # I think this giving excuses # is pretty prevalent, {F uh, } [yo-, +] I work in the school district /

These cases all seem to involve segmentation problems: in (6b), when the speaker says *I remember* it seems that a new thought is starting, which would plausibly correspond to the start of a new slash unit; in the other two cases it would seem preferable to segment into a sequence of two slash units, in case (6c) rather fairly signaled by the hesitation {F uh, } and the restart [yo-, +].

The SWBD-DAMSL tags are composite, and have been characterized as 'tag clusters' (Jurafsky et al., 1997), but different from the composite tags introduced by Popescu-Belis (2008) they do not represent dialogue act combinations. For example, the tag `qw^d` can be decomposed into `q` for question, `w` for WH-, and `^d` for declarative, but only the sub-tag `qw` denotes a communicative function.

The ISO standard is intended to be used for annotating all the communicative functions of dialogue units. The slash units in the Switchboard corpus on average have 1.8 communicative functions, and 62% of the slash units has two or more communicative functions. This means, for the creation of fully-fledged ISO 24617-2 annotations, that in addition to the function tags which can be obtained through the conversion of SWBD-DAMSL tags, further functional tags have to be generated through a more comprehensive interpretation of the dialogues. This is partly possible by interpreting the in-line mark up of certain dialogue phenomena, as discussed in the next section.

3 Interpreting in-line markups

The Switchboard dialogues include the in-line markup (often occurring within slash units) of the following types of disfluencies:

1. restarts, marked up [X + Y] (more detail below);
2. filled pauses, marked up { F ... };
3. explicit editing terms, marked up { E ... };
4. discourse connectives and discourse markers, marked up {C } and {D }.

Asides, such as self-talk and third-person talk, are marked up by means of SWBD-DAMSL tags and are also considered in this Section.

3.1 Restarts and repairs

Following Shriberg (1994), restarts are expressions of the form shown in (7), in which the part RM is called the 'reparandum', a stretch of text to be replaced; RR is the replacing material, and IM is intermediate material (such as a filled pause or an editing term), that separates the two and typically signals that a replacement is going to follow. This is marked up in the Switchboard corpus as shown in (7a).

(7) a. Show me flights [from Boston on + {F uh } from Denver on] Monday
   (RM = from Boston on; IM = {F uh }; RR = from Denver on)

b. **Show me flights** <u>from Boston on *uh*</u> <u>**from Denver on**</u> **Monday**

The ISO 24617-2 annotation makes use of the segmentation shown in (7b), consisting of the segment **Show me flights from Denver on Monday** in the Task dimension, expressing a request; and the segment <u>from Boston on uh from Denver on</u> in the Own Communication Management dimension, expressing a self-correction.

The description of a restart in terms of a 'reparandum' (RM) and replacing material (RR) strongly suggests that restarts are self-corrections.

This is not always correct, however, since the RM part of a restart may be identical to the reparandum, in which case we have a repetition rather than a replacement, and it may be empty; in both cases the ISO 24617-2 definition of a self-correction would not apply. Repetitions often do not signal that the speaker wants to correct what he just said, but rather that he hasn't quite made up his mind yet as to how he wants to express himself, which makes this behaviour a case of stalling, rather than a case of self-correction. In cases where the RR part is empty, the speaker decides not to go on saying what he started to say; this corresponds to what in ISO 24617-2 is called a *retraction*.

Even if the RR part of a restart is not empty and not identical to the reparandum, we do not necessarily have a self-correction, as the examples in (8) show (from sw00-0004, lines 68 and 25, respectively):

(8) a. .. to begin with, [you would -, + you would have,] -

b. .. if they did it [with the + {F uh } just with the] judges, the police have to do..

In such cases, where the reparandum re-appears in the RR part, Meteer & Taylor (1995) speak of an 'insertion'. An insertion has one of the following two forms, where XM denotes the inserted material (and IM may be empty):

(9) a. ... RM IM RM XM ...

b. ... RM IM XM RM ...

In an insertion of the form (9a) the speaker does not so much correct himself; the repetition of the reparandum rather seems to indicate that the speaker needs some time to decide to say what he already started to say; that makes this behaviour a case of stalling rather than self-correction.

The following guideline can be formulated for interpreting the markings of restarts in the Switchboard corpus in terms of the ISO standard :

- if the RR part is empty, then the marked up segment is a Retraction;
- if the RR part is of the form RM XM, then the marked up segment is a Stalling;
- if the RR part is not empty and not of the form RM XM, then the marked up segment is a Self-Correction.

Note that this is no more than a guideline; each individual case has to be inspected in order to be certain about the correct interpretation in the given context.

3.2 Filled pauses

Filled pauses typically signal that the speaker needs a little time to decide how to continue his contribution, and are annotated according to ISO 24617-2 as stalling acts. (The ISO tag 'pausing' is used for those cases where the speaker temporarily suspends the dialogue, as in *just a moment*).

Stalling acts occurring at the beginning of a turn (like *um,* or *well,*) additionally signal that the participant takes the turn; those occurring at the beginning of a slash unit but not at the beginning of a turn (*and* occurs frequently in that position) often indicate that the speaker wants to keep the turn. See further Section 5.2.

Filled pauses may also be indicators of Own Communication Management acts, viz. retractions and self-corrections, or of struggling to find the right words for something and eliciting a collaborative completion (an act in the Partner Communication Management dimension).

3.3 Explicit editing terms

Explicit editing terms are marked up in the Switchboard corpus as { E .... } and often occur after the reparandum part of a restart. In ISO 24617-2 explicit editing terms are regarded as indicators of Own Communication Management acts (a Retraction or as a Self-Correction), or of a Partner Communication Management act (eliciting help); see also Section 3.1.

3.4 Discourse markers

A distinction is made in the Switchboard corpus between 'discourse markers', such as *'Well'* and *'So'*, indicated by { D ... }, and 'coordinating conjunctions', such as *and, but,* and *because*, marked up by { C ... }. In the literature the term 'discourse marker' is commonly understood to include coordinating conjunctions (at utterance level, rather than propositional level), and we follow this convention in this paper.

Discourse markers are important for segmenting a dialogue into meaningful units, since they very often 'bracket' functional segments, and they may also be functional segments on their own. With reference to the AMI corpus, Petukhova & Bunt (2009) have shown that discourse markers are nearly always multifunctional. The most frequently occurring discourse marker, *and*, has an average of 2.6 communicative functions; other frequent ones are *so* (average multifunctionality 2.0); *well* (2.1); *but* (1.9); and *because* (1.2). *And* is used 57% of the time with a small pause as a speaker continuation signal, i.e. as a turn-keeping act; *well* is mostly a turn-taking signal (also mostly with a small pause); *so*, used with or without a small pause, can be both. An example of the characteristic use of *and* is shown in (10), with durations of micro-pauses:

(10) like you said a problem was how many components are in there
(0.28) {C and } (0.12) the power is basically a factor of that
(0.55) {F um } (0.47) {C and } (0.32) this affects you in terms of the size of your device
(0.52) {F um } (0.26) {C and } (0,16) that would have some impact

The importance of discourse markers for segmentation is evidenced in the Switchboard corpus by the fact that an estimated 35% of all slash units begin with a discourse marker. As a discourse marker (rather than a propositional connective), *and* occurs almost exclusively at the start of a slash unit inside a turn; *well* typically occurs in turn-initial position and has a turn-taking or turn-accepting function, as illustrated in (11) (from sw03-0304 line 0087-A049-01).

(11) B: {C So } [what do you, + what kind of hobbies are you] in?/
A: {C Well, } I'm a mother of four, /

Discourse markers may also have a feedback function, a time management function, or a discourse structuring function. Clark and Shaefer (1989) and Clark (1996) claim that *and* has an important feedback function; this claim is not supported by the Switchboard data, where *and* occurs predominantly inside a speaker turn, whereas feedback tends to be expressed at the beginning of a turn.

The markup of discourse markers in the Switchboard corpus is useful for the recognition of slash units; to correctly annotate discourse markers that by themselves have one or more communicative functions according to the ISO 24617-2 standard, a resegmentation is required that treats such occurrences of discourse markers as separate slash units.

3.5 Asides

Asides do have a communicative function, but in a sense do not belong to the dialogue, as (12) illustrates. In the Switchboard corpus, asides like the one in (12) (from sw03-0304, lines 180-A099-01 through 184- A101-02) are annotated with the non-communicative tag't3' (third-party talk).

(12) A: I keep hearing these marvelous things –
B: Yeah, /
B: haven't either. /
A: – about Dear Valley and,
A: {F um, } ⟨to child⟩ {A don't, Adam, } ...

Since an aside typically expresses a dialogue act, it could be annotated with the appropriate communicative function tag(s); moreover, ISO standard annotation includes indicating for each dialogue act the identities of the speaker and the addressee(s); in an aside like the one in in the bottom line in (12) (sw03-0304 line 184), this is possible if the addressee ('Adam') has been introduced in the metadata as one of the participants in the communicative situation.

As for the conversion of Switchboard annotations to the ISO standard, all cases labelled `t3` have to be re-annotated, taking their context of occurrence into account.

4 Phenomena not annotated in Switchboard

4.1 Nonverbal behaviour

Nonverbal behaviour is marked up in-line in Switchboard transcriptions with pointed brackets, and when it occurs as a separate turn it is annotated (even though it is not considered as a slash unit) with the SWBD-DAMSL tag 'x'. An example is seen in the second line of (13) (from dialogue sw03-0304):

(13) sd A: {C so } basically I'm just, ⟨laughter⟩/
x B: ⟨laughter⟩

While marked as being a stretch of nonverbal behaviour, no functional annotation is associated with nonverbal behaviour in the Switchboard corpus, as illustrated by (13) and (14) (line 0014 from dialogue sw00-0004).

(14) sv I think what they need to do is, they need to somehow ⟨lipsmack⟩ take the money out of it. /

The ISO standard makes use of nonverbal and multimodal functional segments besides purely verbal segments (see Petukhova and Bunt, 2012), and supports the functional annotation of such segments

Laughter often expresses a positive emphatic sentiment concerning something that another participant just said, and thus indicates that the laughing participant understood what was said. The appropriate functional ISO tag is thus Auto-Positive (in the Auto-Feedback dimension).

Example (14) would be treated in ISO 24617-2 by distinguishing the discontinuous verbal segment *I think what they need to do is, they need to somehow take the money out of it*, which would be annotated as having the communicative function Inform, and the vocal functional segment defined by its begin and end point being just after the end of *somehow* and before the start of *take*; this segment would be annotated as having a Stalling function. (See ISO 2461702:2012, Annex D, and Petukhova & Bunt, 2012 for more details.)

While `<laughter>` and `<lipsmack>` can mostly be mapped to the ISO function tags Auto-Feedback and Stalling (although each occurrence has to be checked for its function in the context in which it occurs), the addition of these annotations to the Switchboard corpus would require a resegmentation of the dialogues, using functional segments rather than slash units.

4.2 Turn Management

Turn management functions are not annotated in (SWBD-)DAMSL. In the ISO standard they are, the guidelines instructing the annotation of communicative behaviour with turn management functions if and only if a dialogue participant explicitly signals the wish to have or keep the speaker role, or to release it or to give it to another participant. The background of this guideline is that speakers often take the turn simply by starting to speak, like participant B in dialogue fragment (15):

	A:	Anyone wants to add something?
(15)	B:	I would like to add that the controls should be really easy to use.

Any time a dialogue participant (B) starts to speak after another participant (A) has ceased to speak, he (B) can be said to perform a turn-taking (or turn-accepting) act *by implication* of performing a dialogue act which is expressed by what he (B) says.[4] For dialogue act annotation, more interesting are those cases where a speaker *explicitly* indicates that he wants to take on the speaker role, for example by starting to speak without producing any content, such as a filler (*Um,..*) or a discourse marker (e.g. *Well,...* or *You know,....*). The Switchboard examples in (16) illustrate this.

(16) a. (dialogue sw01-0105 lines 01-02)
A: Jimmy, {D so } how do you get most of your news?/
B: {D Well, } [I kind of, + {F uh, } I] watch the national news every day

b. (dialogue sw01-0105 lines 07-08)
A: {D so } when you say the morning news, or evening news or national news is when? /
B: {F Uh, } evening news at six thirty I believe

c. (dialogue sw03-0304 lines 01-02)
A: Tell me what you like to do. /
B: {D Well, } ⟨laughter⟩ [I, +I]] collect antique tools ... /

Whereas stalling when starting to speak is typically a sign of wishing or agreeing to have the speaker role, ceasing to speak while fixating the gaze on another participant (and naming that other participant, especially in multi-party dialogue) is a sign of giving the speaker role to that participant. Slowing down and stalling at the end of an utterance, and a rising intonation, often signals that the speaker wants to keep the speaker role.

Turn management signals are often quite subtle, with an important role being played by nonverbal behaviour accompanying the speech. Since the Switchboard corpus consists of transcriptions of telephone dialogues, the annotation of turn management functions has to be based exclusively on verbal and vocal turn management signals. Turn-initial stallings, slash unit-initial and slash unit-final stallings, and interruptions are the main sources for adding ISO 24617-2 turn management functions to units in the Switchboard corpus. These could be added semi-automatically by identifying the turn-initial, slash-unit initial, and slash-unit final stallings and certain discourse markers, but each individual case would have to be checked for its communicative function in the context in

[4]See Bunt (2011) for a discussion of implications and other semantic relations between dialogue acts.

which it occurs; moreover, a partial resegmentation of the dialogues would be required in order to isolate the units to be annotated with turn-management functions.

4.3 Allo-Feedback

Feedback is communicative behaviour that provides or elicits information about the processing of utterances earlier in a conversation. The ISO standard follows the DIT^{++} annotation scheme in dividing feedback behaviour into those where the speaker provides information about his own processing of previous utterances (Auto-Feedback) and those which provide or elicit information about the addressee's (or addressees') processing (Allo-Feedback). SWBD-DAMSL has tags for annotating Auto-Feedback acts, but not for Allo-Feedback acts.

Examples of Allo-Feedback acts in the Switchboard corpus are shown in (17) line 19 (Switchboard dialogue sw01-0105, lines 0012-A0005-03 to 0019-A0009-01), and in (18) line 66 (from sw00-0004, lines 61-66; in-line markups suppressed):

(17)	12.	A:	I don't, uh, subscribe to cable
	13.	B:	Uh-huh.
	14.	A:	be- because of the poor service and also, uh, because,
	15.	A:	well, I, uh, I give to the United Way
	16.	A:	and so I figured that amount of money I just donate that.
	17.	B:	Uh-huh.
	18.		as opposed to paying for cable.
	19.	A:	Yeah.

In line 18 in (17) B checks the correctness of his understanding of what A said, performing a Check Question (which is commonly expressed by a declarative sentence) in the Auto-Feedback dimension, to which A responds by a confirmation of B's understanding; this constitutes a Confirm act in the Allo-Feedback dimension. The SWBD-DAMSL annotation tags line 18 as `bf` ("Summarize/reformulate") and line 19 as `aa` (Accept/agree), which is not very satisfactory; in line 18 speaker B does neither summarizes nor reformulates something that A has said, but rather adds a consideration to clarify what A said and offers this for confirmation, which A does in line 19, where he does not really express agreement with what B said, but confirms the correctness of his interpretation.

(18)	61.	B:	I've nailed the problem
	62.		but I
	63.	A:	⟨laughter⟩
	64.	B:	⟨laughter⟩
	65.	A:	Leave the details up to someone else, huh?
	66.	B:	Yeah,

In line 65 in (18) A provides a tentative completion of what B was trying to say in line 62, with a check of correctness, to which B replies with an allo-feeback Confirm act. The SWBD-DAMSL annotation tags line 65 as `^2` ("Collaborative Completion") and line 19 as `aa` (Accept/agree). Assigning only `^2` to the slash unit in line 65 fails to account for the *, huh?* part of that unit, which indicates that the speaker is not only performing a completion but also checks the correctness of his understanding on which the completion is based. In line 66 B confirms that correctness, which makes it a Confirm act in the Allo-Feedback dimension.

Identifying the units in the Switchboard dialogues which have an Allo-Feedback function seems quite hard on the basis of the existing SWBD-DAMSL annotations. An important clue is that allo-feedback acts mostly occur in response to allo-feedback acts, but the tagging of auto-feedback acts in the corpus is not very reliable, as example (17) illustrates, and does not seem to provide a solid basis for automatically identifying these acts.

4.4 Communicative function qualifiers

In natural dialogue, speakers often use expressions to qualify their communicative activity for (un)certainty, (un)conditionality, or sentiment. The ISO standard makes use of so-called 'qualifiers' (Petukhova & Bunt, 2010) for representing this in dialogue act annotation. SWBD-DAMSL does not have a device with the same generality, but does use the tag component ^e to express uncertainty (but also other possible qualifications; 'e' stands for elaboration'), as in (19) line 27, and the tag 'am' ('accept maybe/partial accept' - see (19)) line 28, which can be used for some of the cases where ISO 24617-2 uses the qualifier 'uncertain' applied to the communicative function that interprets SWBD-DAMSL's 'accept' tag (which corresponds to a number of more specific tags in the ISO standard).

(19) (dialogue sw03-0304, lines 25-28)

25.	qy	A:	Are you going to move yourwhole family over there then?
26.	nn	B:	No, /
27.	sd ^e		actually, {F uh, } I'm not even sure, /
28.	am	B:	I may, /

In a fully-fledged ISO 24617-2 annotation, it would be necessary to add function qualifiers wherever they apply, including interpretations of the cases where the SWBD-DAMSL tags and tag components'^h' (for 'hold'"), 'am', and ' ^e' are used.

4.5 Relations between dialogue acts

Responsive dialogue acts, such as answers, (dis-)confirmations, (dis-)agreements, acceptance and rejection of offers and requests, acceptance of apologies, return greetings, and so on, all presuppose a particular kind of preceding dialogue act, to which they have a 'functional dependence relation'. The ISO standard annotates these relations in a dialogue; SWBD-DAMSL does not.

Similarly, the ISO standard annotates the relations between a feedback act and the preceding dialogue contribution that the feedback is about, whereas SWBD-DAMSL does not support the annotation of such relations.

Again, in a fully-fledged ISO 24617-2 annotation of the Switchboard dialogues, it would be necessary to add functional and feedback relations wherever they would apply. Examples occur all over the place, for example in (20a) the slash unit in line 155 would be tagged as an answer that is linked to the question in line 153 by a 'functional dependence' relation, and in (20b) the feedback utterance in line 80 is tagged as an 'autoPositive' act that is linked to the preceding Inform by a 'feedback dependence' relation.

(20) a. (dialogue sw03-0304, lines 153-155)

153.	B:	[You guys, + are you guys] getting snow?
154.	A:	We, - /
155.		it is snowing right now. /

b. (dialogue sw03-0304, lines 79-80)

79.	A:	{C so, } it's been a real interesting thing for them ../
80.	B:	That's great. /

The addition of functional and feedback dependence relations to Switchboard annotations can probably be done semi-automatically, because of the following regularities that govern the dependency relations:

- for functional dependence:
  - these occur (always) for a particular set of dialogue act types, the 'responsive' ones, which are specified in the ISO standard;
  - for each type of responsive dialogue act the 'functional antecedent' is a dialogue act with a specific communicative function (like the functional antecedent of a Confirm being a Check Question) and a specific speaker;
  - the functional antecedent of a responsive dialogue act is nearly always the most recent dialogue act of the appropriate type (Petukhova et al., 2011).
- for feedback dependence:
  - these occur (always) for dialogue acts in one of the two feedback dimensions;
  - the 'antecedent' of a feedback act is in the vast majority of cases either the most recent dialogue act contributed by the previous speaker, or a subdialogue that ends there, intervening dialogue acts being mainly turn management acts, time management acts, and own communication management acts. In the latter case it may be difficult, however, to (automatically) determine the start of such a subdialogue.

5 Discussion and Conclusions

A comparison of annotation schemes is often thought of as comparing the respective typologies of dialogue acts and their encodings, but we have seen in this paper that the construction of ISO 24617-2 annotations for the dialogues in the Switchboard corpus, starting from the existing SWBD-DAMSL tagging, is much more complicated than that. Fang et al. (2012) have shown that the replacement of SWBD-DAMSL tags by ISO 24617-2 communicative functions can be done automatically for 84% of the Switchboard corpus, which is a promising start. In this paper we addressed the following additional aspects of adding fully-fledged ISO 24617-2 annotations to the Switchboard corpus:

1. The ISO standard is intended for annotating all the communicative functions of dialogue units in the nine dimensions defined in the standard. The slash units in the Switchboard corpus have only one functional tag from the SWBD-DAMSL scheme, while on average they would have 1.8 communicative functions according to ISO 24617-2. This means that the number of functional tags in the corpus should be almost doubled. In some cases it is possible to derive the appropriate ISO tags from in-line markups (see 2, 3, and 7); in other cases this does not seem feasible (see 4, 5, 6, and 8). In nearly all cases, the addition of communicative functions requires the dialogues to be partly re-segmented, using the more fine-grained DIT^{++} segmentation of dialogues into functional segments.

2. The in-line markup of restarts, repairs, and edit terms in the Switchboard corpus can be replaced semi-automatically by functional annotations in the ISO dimension of Own Communication Management, making use of the markup to automatically resegment the slash units in which these markups occur. The results must be manually checked, however, since edit terms and repetitions sometimes have other functions, e.g. as indicators of dialogue acts in the Partner Communication Management dimension.

3. The in-line markups of filled pauses can be used to resegment the utterances in which they occur, and to annotate these segments with TIme Management functions. This can be done automatically with manual checks, since filled pauses can have functions in other dimensions than Time Management.

4. Discourse markers, as marked up in-line in the Switchboard corpus, have to be identified as separate functional segments if they express one or more dialogue acts by themselves. Their communicative functions cannot be derived from the Switchboard tagging, and require a re-annotation taking their context of occurrence into consideration.

5. Asides, such as third-party talk, have communicative functions just like other functional segments (and slash units), which can only be constructed through re-annotation with the ISO 24617-2 scheme.

6. Stretches of nonverbal communicative behaviour, such as laughter, chuckles, sighs, and lip smacks, should be treated as functional segments not only when they occur as a separate turn, but also when they occur inside a slash unit; their ISO 24617-2 annotation cannot be derived from the Switchboard markups.

7. Turn Management functions can be added semi-automatically to Switchboard once discourse markers have been treated as indicated in 4 and filled pauses as in 3, if detailed information is available about small pauses associated with turn-initial, segment-initial and segment-final discourse markers and filled pauses.

8. The addition of Allo-Feedback functions to Switchboard can partly be done automatically by identifying responsive dialogue acts that respond to a dialogue act in the Auto-Feedback dimension. The SWBD-DAMSL tagging is very crude in indicating dimensions, however; the tag component `^c` is used to represent “about communication”, so an Auto-Feedback Check Question could be tagged as `qd^c`, but this has not been done systematically in the Switchboard corpus (moreover, there is no SWBD-DAMSL tag corresponding exactly to ISO’s Check Question). In the absence of detailed encodings of functions in the Auto-Feedback dimension, it hardly seems feasible to derive Allo-Feedback functions automatically.

9. The ISO communicative function qualifiers for (un-)certainty and (un-)conditionality have no counterparts in SWBD-DAMSL; the tags and tag components ‘^h’, ‘am’, `` `^e' `` can be used to automatically identify cases which are relevant to examine.

10. The functional and feedback relations that form an important part of the ISO 24617-

2 annotation of a dialogue can be added largely automatically for functional dependences, since these relations are known to occur always (and only) for certain types of dialogue acts (the 'responsive' ones) and nearly always relate to the most recent dialogue act of a specific type performed by the previous speaker. For feedback relations, similarly a good guess that could be used in a semi-automatic process is to take the last dialogue act performed by the previous speaker. Manual checks are needed to verify the correctness of the relations generated in this way, especially for feedback dependence relations, which may have a wider scope (for details see Petukhova et al., 2011).

With respect to the resegmentation and reannotation that several of these aspects necessitate, it may be noted that Petukhova and Bunt (2011) have developed a highly successful machine-learning based approach for the automatic segmentation and annotation of raw spoken dialogue. A variant of this method could conceivably be defined for the ISO-compliant resegmentation and reannotation of Switchboard dialogues that makes use of the information encoded in the Switchboard transcriptions, in particular in the in-line markups.

Acknowledgement

The research described in this article was supported in part by grants received from the General Research Fund of the Research Grants Council of the Hong Kong Special Administrative Region, China (RGC Project No. 142711) and City University of Hong Kong (Project Nos 7002793, 9610226, 9041694, 9610188, and 7008062). The authors would like to acknowledge the academic input and the technical support received from the members of the Dialogue Systems Group (http://dsg.ctl.cityu.edu.hk) based at the Department of Chinese, Translation and Linguistics, City University of Hong Kong

References

Allen, J. and M. Core (1997). *DAMSL: Dialogue Act Markup in Several Layers (Draft 2.1). Technical Report*. Rochester, NY: University of Rochester.

Bunt, H. (2009). The DIT++ taxonomy for functional dialogue act markup. In D. Heylen, C. Pelachaud, R. Catizone, and D. Traum (Eds.), *Proceedings of EDAML–AAMAS Workshop "Towards a Standard Markup Language for Embodied Dialogue Acts", Budapest*, pp. 13–24.

Bunt, H. (2011). Multifunctionality in dialogue. *Computer, Speech and Language 25*(2), 225 – 245.

Bunt, H., J. Alexandersson, J. Carletta, J.-W. Choe, A. Fang, K. Hasida, K. Lee, V. Petuhova, A. Popescu-Belis, L. Romary, and D. Soria, C. Traum (2010). Towards an ISO standard for dialogue act annotation. In *Proceedings Seventh International Conference on Language Resources and Evaluation (LREC 2010),*, Malta.

Bunt, H., J. Alexandersson, J.-W. Choe, A. Fang, K. Hasida, V. Petuhova, A. Popescu-Belis, and D. Traum (2012). Iso 24617-2: A semantically-based standard for dialogue annotation. In *Proceedings Eighth International Conference on Language Resources and Evaluation (LREC 2012)*, Istanbul.

Clark, H. (1996). *Using Language*. Cambridge, UK: Cambridge University Press.

Clark, H. and E. Shaefer (1989). Contributing to discourse. *Cognitive Science 13*, 259–294.

Core, M. and J. Allen (1997). Coding dialogs with the DAMSL annotation schema. In *AAAI Fall Symposium on Communicative Action in Humans and Machines*, Boston, MA.

Fang, A., H. Bunt, J. Cao, and X. Liu (2011). Relating the semantics of dialogue acts to linguistic properties: A machine learning perspective through lexical cues. In *Proceedings 5th IEEE International Conference on Semantic Computing*, Stanford University, Palo Alto.

Fang, A., H. Bunt, J. Cao, and X. Liu (2012). The annotation of the Switchboard corpus with the new iso standard for dialogue act analysis. In *Proceedings 8th Joint ISO-ACL SIGSEM Workshop on Interoperable Semantic Annotation (ISA-8)*, Pisa.

Geertzen, J., V. Petukhova, and H. Bunt (2007). A multidimensional approach to utterance segmentation and dialogue act classification. In *Proceedings of the 8th SIGdial Workshop on Discourse and Dialogue*, Antwerp, pp. 140–149.

Jurafsky, D., E. Shriberg, and D. Biasca (1997). *Switchboard SWBD-DAMSL Shallow-Discourse-Annotation Coders Manual.* Available at http://stripe.colorado.edu/.

Meteer and R. A. Taylor (1995). *Dysfluency annotation stylebook for the Switchboard corpus.* ftp://ftp.cis.upenn.edu/pub/treebank/swbd/docs/DFL-book.ps.

Petukhova, V. and H. Bunt (2009). Towards a multidimensional semantics of discourse markers in spoken dialogue. In *Proceedings of the Eighth International Workshop on Computational Semantics (IWCS-8)*, Tilburg, the Netherlands, pp. 157–168.

Petukhova, V. and H. Bunt (2010). Introducing communicative function qualifiers. In *Proceedings Second International Conference on Global Interoperability for Language resources (ICGL-2), Hong Kong*, pp. 123 – 131.

Petukhova, V. and H. Bunt (2011). Incremental dialogue act understanding. In *Proceedings Ninth International Conference on Computational Semantics (IWCS 2011), Oxford*, pp. 235 – 244.

Petukhova, V. and H. Bunt (2012). The coding and annotation of multimodal dialogue acts. In *Proceedings Eighth International Conference on Language Resources and Evaluation (LREC 2012),*, Istanbul.

Petukhova, V., L. Prévot, and H. Bunt (2011). Multi-level discourse relations between dialogue units. In *Proceedings 6th Joint ACL-ISO Workshop on Interoperable Semantic Annotation (ISA-6), Oxford*, pp. 18–27.

Popescu-Belis, A. (2008). Dimensionality of dialogue act tagsets. *Language Resources and Evaluation 14*, 99–107.

Shriberg, E. (1994). *Preliminaries to a theory of speech disfluencies.* Ph.D. Thesis, University of Berkeley.

Annotation for annotation
– Toward eliciting implicit linguistic knowledge through annotation –
(Project Note)

Tokunaga Takenobu **Iida Ryu** **Mitsuda Koh**
Department of Computer Science
Tokyo Institute of Technology
{take, ryu-i}@cl.cs.titech.ac.jp, mitsuda.k.aa@m.titech.ac.jp

Abstract

The last two decades witnessed a great success of revived empiricism in NLP research. However, there are still several NLP tasks that are not successful enough. As one of many directions for going beyond the revived empiricism, this paper introduces a project for annotating annotations with annotators' rationales behind them. As a first step of this enterprise, the paper particularly focuses on data collection during the annotation and discusses their potential uses. Finally a preliminary experiment for data collection is described with the data analysis.

1 Introduction

The last two decades witnessed a great success of revived empiricism in NLP research. Namely, the *corpus construction and machine learning* (CC-ML) approach has been the main stream of NLP research, where corpora are annotated for a specific task and then they are used as training data for machine learning (ML) techniques to build a system for the task.

The CC-ML approach has been expected to remedy the notorious knowledge construction bottleneck in traditional rule-based approaches. In the rule-based approach, given a specific task (e.g. POS tagging), human experts (e.g. computational linguists) create rules covering various linguistic phenomena based on their insight. In contrast, in the CC-ML approach, human experts mainly focus on creating annotation guidelines. According to the guidelines, annotation is usually performed by a number of annotators who do not necessarily have deep linguistic knowledge, aiming at increasing the corpus size. Resultant large annotated corpora are expected to cover broader linguistic phenomena in terms of a collection of annotation instances than the expert-constructed rules in a rule-based approach. Regularities corresponding to the rules are extracted from the annotated corpora by the ML techniques.

The primacy of the CC-ML approach over the rule-based approach has been shown in fundamental NLP tasks (e.g. POS tagging, syntactic parsing and word sense disambiguation) as well as in various applications (e.g. information extraction, machine translation and summarisation) through prevalent competition-type conferences. However, too much dominance of the revived empiricism has recently worried a number of researchers (Reiter, 2007; Steedman, 2008; Krahmer, 2010; Church, 2011). For instance, Church (2011), who is one of the initiators of the revived empiricism, warned us that we should follow the CC-ML approach with an awareness of the limitations of the underlying ML techniques.

One of the problems of the CC-ML approach is that the annotated information in the corpora is often limited to the output for a given specific task. Together with other clues (e.g. POS of surrounding words of a target), a system for the task is built by using ML techniques. However, the validity of these clues has been rarely examined deeply. This would be because the annotator's decision process has attracted less attention than the resultant annotations themselves. Therefore, there have been few attempts to systematically collect the annotator's rationales behind the annotation process.

From an engineering viewpoint, a machine does not need to perform a task in the same manner as a human does. The currently used clues might be sufficient for doing the job even though a human uses different information. For instance, POS tagging and parsing are successful instances of the CC-ML approach. However, this approach does not always work well on other tasks such as semantic and discourse processing. For instance, the performance of the state-of-the-art coreference resolution model still stays around 0.7 in F-score (Haghighi and Klein, 2010). Furthermore, the performance of zero anaphora resolution in Japanese is much worse, around 0.4 in F-score (Iida and Poesio, 2011). Such relatively low performance suggests that some crucial information should have been utilised for ML techniques.

Against this background, we propose annotating each annotation with the annotator's rationale behind her/his decision. Since the rationale explains the validity of the annotation instance, it can be considered as a kind of meta-level annotation against the object-level annotation rather than a mere attribute of the annotation. We expect that analysing these rationales behind human decisions reveals more effective information for a given task that has never been used by existing ML techniques. We believe this is one of the ways to integrate the revived empiricism and rationalism.

As a first step of this enterprise, this paper particularly discusses what kinds of information can be collected during the annotation process for estimating a rationale behind each annotation decision. We also explain potential uses of the collected information. Finally, we describe our preliminary experiment for collecting the annotator's actions and eye-gaze during her/his annotation process.

2 Data to collect

For the analysis of the annotator's rationales, we plan to collect two types of data, *overt* and *covert* data, which complement each other. The overt data are observable ones including the annotator's actions such as keystrokes, mouse clicks and dragging, and her/his eye-gaze. In contrast, the covert data reside in the annotator's mental process, i.e. her/his thoughts, which can not be observed directly.

Collecting overt data requires some specialised equipment. For collecting the annotator's actions we need annotation tools that can record every input. In addition, recent eye tracking devices enable us to capture an annotator's eye movement quite precisely at high frequency. This equipment enables us to capture the annotator's observable behaviour to a large extent. Such automatically collected low-level data can be further translated into more interpretable abstract actions and objects, which should be defined with respect to the annotation task. For instance, when annotating predicate-argument relations, mouse operations should be translated to meaningful actions like identifying text spans (e.g. words, phrases) corresponding to predicates and arguments, and identifying the relations between them. Likewise, the eye-gaze should be translated to the corresponding text span that the annotator looked at, and together with their time stamps they are further translated to fixations on the text spans. By analysing the temporal relations of these abstract actions, we can reveal what text spans the annotator looks at prior to establishing a predicate-argument relation. Such a prior glance at a certain text span is usually performed unconsciously but will be an important clue for analysing the annotator's decision process. Note that this sort of information is difficult to capture by TAP which is described below. In addtion, collecting overt data has the advantage that it does not interfere with the annotation process.

In order to collect verbalised rationales, which is difficult to draw out from the overt data, we could adopt the think-aloud protocol (TAP) (Ericsson and Simon, 1984), which enforces annotators to explain aloud their decision process. Although TAP makes the annotator's covert thoughts explicit, it increases her/his cognitive load, thus interferes with her/his natural annotation task. In order to decrease their cognitive load, we would make dyads to annotate corpora collaboratively and record their dialogues, expecting that we can extract clues of the annotators' decision process from their utterances. This method might be less effective to draw out their rationales for annotation than the TAP, but as dialogue is a natural act for collaboration, the annotators' cognitive load would be less than the TAP.

3 Potential uses of the collected data

The following are potential uses of the collected data.

Finding useful information for NLP
Given a certain task, the collected data would give some hints to understand human decision processes. Therefore, the information can be useful for replicating human decisions by using ML-based approaches.

Evaluating annotation quality
The quality of corpora is often evaluated based on the agreement ratio and the κ coefficient (Carletta, 1996) between multiple annotators. Analysing the collected data would help to estimate the realiability of each annotation instance. For instance, the long annotation time for an instance is an indication of its difficulty, therefore the annotation on such an instance might be less reliable.

Evaluating and training annotators
Unlike the quality of corpora, the quality of annotators is rarely discussed. In addition to the extent to which annotators can replicate the gold standard annotation (result-based metric), the collected data can be used for evaluating annotators by comparing their behaviours with that of expert annotators. This is a process-based metric, thus can be more informative for training annotators by identifying the differences of their behaviour.

4 Preliminary experiment – collecting actions and eye-gaze during annotation –

4.1 Materials

We conducted a preliminary experiment for collecting an annotator's actions and eye-gaze during her/his annotation of predicate-argument relations in Japanese texts. Given a text in which candidates of predicates and arguments were marked beforehand in the annotation tool, the annotators were instructed to add links between correct predicate-argument pairs by using the keyboard and mouse. We distinguished three types of links based on the case marker of arguments, i.e. *ga* (nominative), *o* (accusative) and *ni* (dative). For elliptical arguments of a predicate, which are quite common in Japanese texts, their antecedents were linked to the predicate. Since the candidates were marked based on the automatic output of a parser, some candidates did not have their counterparts.

We recruited three annotators who had experiences of annotating predicate-argument relations. Each annotator was assigned 43 texts for annotation, which were the same across the annotators. These 43 texts were selected from a Japanese balanced corpus (BCCWJ) (Maekawa et al., 2010). Considering capturing eye-gaze, we prohibited scrolling a text during annotation. Thus, the texts were truncated to about 1,000 characters so that they fit into the text area of the annotation tool.

We employed a multi-purpose annotation tool *Slate* (Kaplan et al., 2012) with necessary modifications, particularly by implementing a logging function for capturing an annotator's input.

Annotator's gaze was captured by the Tobii T60 eye tracker at intervals of 1/60 second. The display size was $1,280 \times 1,024$ pixels and the distance between the display and the annotator's eye was maintained at about 50 cm. In order to minimise the head movement, we used a chin rest.

4.2 Agreement ratio and annotation time

The number of annotated links between predicates and arguments by three annotators A_0, A_1 and A_2 were 3,353 (A_0), 3,764 (A_1) and 3,462 (A_2) respectively. There were several cases where the annotator added multiple links with the same link type to a predicate, e.g. in case of conjunctive arguments; we excluded these instances for simplicity in the analysis below. The number of the remaining links were 3,054 (A_0), 3,251 (A_1) and 2,996 (A_2) respectively. These annotation instances were used for analysing the relation between the agreement ratio and annotation time of the annotated links.

Having fixed a predicate and link type (case marker) pair, we considered the extent to which the annotators agreed on its argument. Among 2,209 predicate and link type pairs that all three annotators annotated, the three agreed in 1,952 pairs. Thus, the agreement ratio of the annotation among three was 0.884. When allowing agreement by only two annotators, the average of pairwise agreement ratios increased to 0.902.

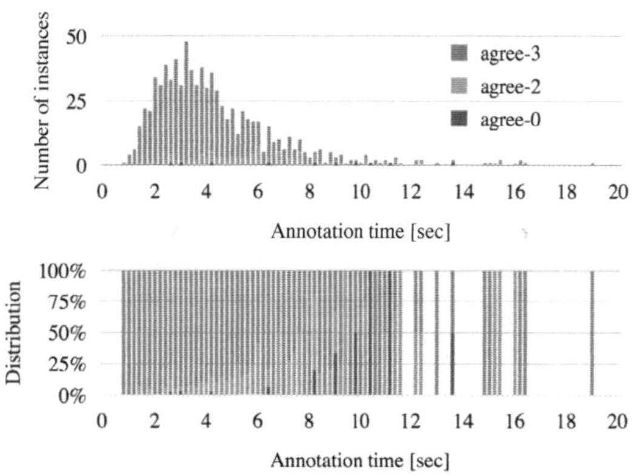

Figure 1: Relation between annotation time and agreement

The annotation time for a link is defined as the time duration from the onset of the first gaze fixation on the predicate after the previous link establishment until the establishment of the current link. The fixation is detected by the Dispersion-Threshold Identification (I-DT) algorithm (Salvucci and Goldberg, 2000) with the space margin of 16 pixels and the time window of 100 msec.

Figure 1 (upper) shows the relation between the average annotation time of the annotators (x-axis with interval width in 0.5 sec) and the number of agreed instances (y-axis). The agreed instances are further divided into three cases: agreed by three (agree-3), agreed by two (agree 2) and no agreement (agree-0). Figure 1 (lower) shows the distribution of the degree of agreement in each interval. The figures indicate that taking longer annotation time suggests difficulty of the annotation instance, thus its low reliability. This tendency indicates that we would be able to estimate the reliability of annotations without the gold standard nor any counterpart for calculating agreement metrics.

5 Related work

We here focus on related work utilising eye-tracking data. As for the analysis of dialogue data, numerous studies on dialogue research could be useful.

Recent development of the eye-tracking technology enables various research fields to employ eye-gaze data, including psycholinguistics and problem solving (Duchowski, 2002). There have been a number of studies on the relations between eye-gaze and language comprehension/production (Griffin and Bock, 2000; Richardson et al., 2007). Compared to the studies on language and eye-gaze, the role of gaze in general problem solving settings has been less studied (Bednarik and Tukiainen, 2008; Rosengrant, 2010; Tomanek et al., 2010). Since our current interest, corpus annotation, can be considered as a problem solving as well as language comprehension, various existing metrics derived from eye-tracking data would be useful.

Rosengrant (2010) proposed an analysis method named *gaze scribing* where eye-tracking data is combined with subjects thought process derived by the TAP, underlining the importance of applying gaze scribing to various problem solving.

Tomanek et al. (2010) utilised eye-tracking data to evaluate difficulties of named entities for selecting training instances for active learning techniques. Our analysis in the previous section is similar to theirs in that the annotator's gaze is used for estimating the annotation difficulty. However, our annotation task is more complex (named entity recognition vs. predicate-argument relations), and in a more natural setting, meaning that all possible relations in a text were annotated in a single session in our setting, while each session targeted a single named entity (NE) instance in a limited context in the setting of Tomanek et al. (2010). Due to such a more realistic setting, the definition of the annotation time is not obvious in our case. Furthermore our fixation target is more precise, i.e. words, rather than a coarse area around the target NE.

6 Concluding remarks

This paper proposed annotating annotations with the annotator's rationales during the annotation process. We particularly discussed overt and covert data collection during the annotation and potential uses of the collected data. Results of a preliminary data collection and the data analysis were also shown. The project has just started. We need to collect more data, both overt and covert, and to establish a method to explore the human annotation process by analysing the interaction between both kinds of data. We believe the direction proposed in the present paper is one of the ways for going beyond the revived empiricism in the study of language processing.

References

Roman Bednarik and Markku Tukiainen. 2008. Temporal eye-tracking data: Evolution of debugging strategies with multiple representations. In *Proceedings of the 2008 symposium on Eye tracking research & applications (ETRA '08)*, pages 99–102.

Jean Carletta. 1996. Assessing agreement on classification tasks: The kappa statistic. *Computational Linguistics*, 22(2):249–254.

Kenneth Church. 2011. A pendulum swung too far. *Linguistic Issues in Language Technology*, 6(5):1–27.

Andrew T. Duchowski. 2002. A breadth-first survey of eye-tracking applications. *Behavior Research Methods, Instruments, and Computers*, 34(4):455–470.

K. Anders Ericsson and Herbert A. Simon. 1984. *Protocol Analysis – Verbal Reports as Data –*. The MIT Press.

Zenzi M. Griffin and Kathryn Bock. 2000. What the eyes say about speaking. *Psychological Science*, 11(4):274–279.

Aria Haghighi and Dan Klein. 2010. Coreference resolution in a modular, entity-centered model. In *Human Language Technologies: The 2010 Annual Conference of the North American Chapter of the Association for Computational Linguistics*, pages 385–393.

Ryu Iida and Massimo Poesio. 2011. A cross-lingual ILP solution to zero anaphora resolution. In *Proceedings of the 49th Annual Meeting of the Association for Computational Linguistics: Human Language Technologies (ACL-HLT 2011)*, pages 804–813.

Dain Kaplan, Ryu Iida, Kikuko Nishina, and Takenobu Tokunaga. 2012. Slate – a tool for creating and maintaining annotated corpora. *Journal for Language Technology and Computational Linguistics*, 26(2):89–101.

Emiel Krahmer. 2010. What computational linguists can learn from psychologists (and vice versa). *Computational Linguistics*, 36(2):285–294.

Kikuo Maekawa, Makoto Yamazaki, Takehiko Maruyama, Masaya Yamaguchi, Hideki Ogura, Wakako Kashino, Toshinobu Ogiso, Hanae Koiso, and Yasuharu Den. 2010. Design, compilation, and preliminary analyses of balanced corpus of contemporary written Japanese. In *Proceedings of the Eigth International Conference on Language Resources and Evaluation (LREC 2010)*, pages 1483–1486.

Ehud Reiter. 2007. The shrinking horizons of computational linguistics. *Computational Linguistics*, 33(2):283–287.

Daniel C. Richardson, Rick Dale, and Michael J. Spivey. 2007. Eye movements in language and cognition: A brief introduction. In Monica Gonzalez-Marquez, Irene Mittelberg, Seana Coulson, and Michael J. Spivey, editors, *Methods in Cognitive Linguistics*, pages 323–344. John Benjamins.

David Rosengrant. 2010. Gaze scribing in physics problem solving. In *Proceedings of the 2010 symposium on Eye tracking research & applications (ETRA '10)*, pages 45–48.

Dario D. Salvucci and Joseph H. Goldberg. 2000. Identifying fixations and saccades in eye-tracking protocols. In *Proceedings of the 2000 symposium on Eye tracking research & applications (ETRA '00)*, pages 71–78.

Mark Steedman. 2008. On becoming a discipline. *Computational Linguistics*, 34(1):137–144.

Katrin Tomanek, Udo Hahn, Steffen Lohmann, and Jürgen Ziegler. 2010. A cognitive cost model of annotations based on eye-tracking data. In *Proceedings of the 48th Annual Meeting of the Association for Computational Linguistics (ACL 2010)*, pages 1158–1167.

Inference Patterns with Intensional Adjectives

James Pustejovsky
Brandeis University
jamesp@cs.brandeis.edu

Abstract

In this paper we report on an ongoing multi-institution effort to encode inferential patterns associated with adjective modification in English. We focus here on a subset of intensional adjectives typically referred to as "non-subsective" predicates. This class includes adjectives such as *alleged*, *supposed*, *so-called*, and related modally subordinating predicates. We discuss the initial results of corpus-based investigations to discriminate the patterns of inference associated with these adjectives. Based on these studies, we have created an initial annotation specification that we are using to create a corpus of adjective-related inferences in English.

1 Introduction

One of the primary goals for linguistic annotation projects is the explicit representation of the syntactic and semantic information necessary for the creation of useful and meaningful inferential structures. In this brief note, we report on a multi-institution effort underway to identify and model the inferential patterns associated with three diverse classes of adjectives in English. This research combines the efforts of Princeton Univeristy (C. Fellbaum), Stanford University (A. Zaenen and L. Karttunen), and Brandeis University (the present author).

Adjectives can be divided into different classes, depending on what dimensions of analysis are being used. Classic semantic field analysis (cf. (Dixon, 1991; Lyons, 1977; Raskin and Nirenburg, 1995)) categorizes the attributes denoted by adjectives according to a thematic organization, centered around a human frame-of-reference, as lexically encoded in the language, such the following classes:[1] DIMENSION, PHYSICAL PROPERTY, COLOR, EMOTIONS, TEMPORAL SPATIAL VALUE, MANNER.

As intuitive as these classes might be for organizing aspects of the lexis of a language, they fail to provide a coherent guide to the inferential patterns associated with adjectival modification. An alternative approach is to adopt a conceptually conservative but more formally descriptive and operational distinction, one which groups adjectives into inferential classes. (Amoia and Gardent, 2006) and (Amoia et al., 2008), following (Kamp, 1975) and (Kamp and Partee, 1995), make just such a move, adopting a four class distinction based on inferential properties of the adjective, as illustrated below:

(1) In the construction, [A N], A can be classed as:
a. INTERSECTIVE: the object described is both A and N.
b. SUBSECTIVE: the object described is A relative to the set of N, but not independent of N.
c. PRIVATIVE: the object described is not an N, by virtue of A.
d. NON-SUBSECTIVE: there is epistemic uncertainty whether the object is N.

These constructions constitute patterns that license specific inferences associated with classes of adjectives, and can be exploited in the context of text-based inference systems, such as the RTE (Amoia and Gardent, 2006). This classification, however, is both too broadly defined to model the finer inferential distinctions within each class, and too narrow

[1] It should be noted that (Raskin and Nirenburg, 1995), however, also discuss inferential patterns for distinct classes.

to include the behavior of other adjective classes, in particular, those taking clausal complements. For these reasons, we have chosen to study three different classes of adjectives that require refinements and additions to the inference patterns given above. These classes are:

(2) a. Scalar adjectives: both dimensional (*big, small*) and evaluative (*happy, pretty*) scalars have been categorized as subsective adjectives;

b. Adjectives with clausal complements: adjectives such as *annoying* and *nice*, when governing clausal complements, do not fit nicely into any of the above classes;

c. Intensional adjectives: adjectives such as *alleged* and *supposed* are non-subsective, but in complex ways that are dependent on the semantics of the nominal head.

Concerning the third adjective class, the intensional adjectives, the effect of modifying the nominal head is the introduction of epistemic uncertainty regarding the description.

(3) T: The police arrested the **alleged** criminal.

H: A criminal was arrested.

Hence, this inference would be false. Now consider the pair below:

(4) T: Archeologists discovered an **alleged** paleolithic stone tool.

H: A stone tool was discovered.

This inference is legitimate because the epistemic scope of the adjective *alleged* is the adjective *paleolithic*, and not the nominal head itself. In the next section, we look at the behavior of the non-subsective intensional adjectives in more detail, and see that there is a more nuanced, but still systematic, pattern at work.

2 Intensional Adjective Behavior

Recall that intersective adjectives such as *carnivorous* have the following behavior:

(5) $\|A\ N\| = \|A\| \cap \|N\|$

Subsective adjectives, on the other hand, such as *big*, can be modeled as follows:

(6) $\|A\ N\| \subseteq \|N\|$

The intensional adjectives can be split into privatives and non-subsective. Privatives, such as *fake* or *pretend*, can be analyzed as follows:

(7) $\|A\ N\| \cap \|N\| = \emptyset$

Intensional non-subsective adjectives introduce an epistemic uncertainty for the elements within their scope. Examples of this class include *alleged*, *supposed*, and *presumed*, and they call into question some predicative property of the nouns they modify. Following (Kamp and Partee, 1995), no informative inference is associated with this construction:

(8) a. $[A\ N]$ (alleged criminal)

b. $\not\models N$

However, contrary to what is claimed in (Amoia and Gardent, 2006), non-subsective adjectives do appear to license specific inferences when examined in a broader context than the [A N] construction usually studied. From preliminary corpus studies of this class[2], several distinct patterns of inference emerge. While the typical resulting composition entails uncertainty of whether the nominal head belongs to the mentioned sortal, (9a) below, there are many contexts where the epistemic scope is reduced to a modification or additional attribution of the nominal head, as shown in (9b).

(9) a. The **alleged criminal** fled the country.

b. Archeologists discovered an **alleged paleolithic tool**.

In Example (9a), the adjective *alleged* calls into question the predicative property of 'criminality' of the *criminal*. When a predicative property is called into question by adjectives of this class, are there any systematic inferences to be made about the semantic field? E.g., is the semantic field still guaranteed to be some hypernym of *criminal*? Even if the individual does not belong to the set of "criminals", it does still seem to belong to the set of "persons". In example (9b), contrastively, at least under one interpretation, it is whether the *tool* is *paleolithic* or not that is called into question: i.e., the object belongs to the set of "tools" regardless if it is truly *paleolithic* or not.[3] This inference is schematically represented below.

[2]The initial corpus has been collected from directed CQL queries over two Sketch Engine corpora, Ententen12 and BNC. Three sentence "snippets" have been compiled from this source.

[3]One reviewer has correctly pointed out that this inference still appears too weak to capture the intended interpretation.

(10) Given the construction $[A_{int}\ N]$, where A_{int} is *alleged*, ..., then:
a. $[A_{int}\ N] \not\models N$
b. $[A_{int}\ A_2\ N] \not\models A_2$
c. $[A_{int}\ A_2\ N] \models N$

Such an inference pattern is subject to contextual variables, many of which are not available to sentential compositional mechanisms, but some constraints can be identified. For example, the closer the head noun is to a sortal base level category, such as *bird*, *table*, or *tool*, the more likely the inference in (10b) will go through. Consider the examples below:

(11) a. The store bought an alleged antique vase.
b. The researcher found an alleged Mozart sonata.

These cases make it clear that the epistemic uncertainty in (11) involves an additional aspect of the NP, beyond the unassailable characteristics of the entailed head. That is, the object is clearly a vase (in (11a)) and demonstrably a sonata (in (10b)). Such evidence, however, will not always be available within the composition of a sentence, but will be derivable from context (if at all). We will refer to the canonical inference in (10a) as the "Wide-scope reading", and the inferences in (10b-c) as the "Narrow-scope reading".

Another interesting distinction emerging in the basic [A N] construction with intensional adjectives is one based on the type of the nominal head. The most common semantic types occuring in the corpus are shown below, along with apparent scoping behavior.

(12) a. EVENT NOMINAL: *violation*, *misconduct*, *murder*, *assault*. The more specific nominal descriptions carry greater inferential force for the hypernym. That is, *murder* suggests inference of a death.
b. AGENTIVE NOUN: *collaborator*, *perpetrator*, *murderer*, *criminal*. Epistemic scope is over the entire sortal. The canonical form, "the alleged criminal".
c. UNDERGOER NOUN: *victim*. While not always the case, the scope is narrowed to a modification of the event: For example, "the alleged victims of Whitey Bulger".

Consider the sentences in (13), where *alleged* is modifying an event nominal.

(13) a. He denies the alleged assault on the police.
b. The greatest number of alleged violations occurred in California.
c. He's been charged in connection with the alleged murder of John Smith, whose mutilated body ...

The inferences associated with (13a-b) follow from the template in (10a). For sentence (13c), however, we need to infer that there was, in fact, a killing, although it is uncertain whether it was a murder. This requires the inference rule below, where the hypernym of the event nominal is infererable from the context.

(14) Given the construction $[A_{int}\ N]$, where N is an event nominal, with certain feature, then:
a. $[A_{int}\ N] \not\models N$
$\models N'$ where $N \subseteq N'$

We refer to this inference rule as the "Hypernym reading". Similar remarks hold for undergoer nominals in some contexts, where the scope of the intensional adjective can be lowered to a modification of the event description. This is illustrated below, in (15b).

(15) a. Testimony will be heard from the alleged victim in court.
b. The families of two alleged victims of James "Whitey" Bulger have received compensation.

Sentence (15a) behaves according to the canonical template, while (15b) involves a narrower scope of the epistemic uncertainty. That is, the inference should be made that there are victims, but the cause (or etiology) of this designation is uncertain. This rule is formally related to that presented above in (10), where the modification (argument specification, in fact) is postnominal.

(16) Given the construction $[A_{int}\ N\ XP_{mod}]$, where XP_{mod} is a modification or argument, then:
a. $[A_{int}\ N\ XP_{mod}] \not\models N\ XP_{mod}$
c. $[A_{int}\ N\ XP_{mod}] \models N$

Certainly more is intended than a mere hypernymic assertion, including the associated presuppositions of the context variables introducing the allegation and the epistemic uncertainty itself. These are issues presently being explored.

Summarizing the semantic behavior for this class, we have identified at least three distinct structure-to-inference mappings associated with intensional (non-subsective) adjectives. These are:

(17) Structure-to-Inference Mappings:
a. Wide-scope reading:
$[A_{int}\ N] \nvDash N$
b. Narrow-scope reading 1:
$[A_{int}\ A_2\ N] \nvDash A_2, \vDash N$
c. Narrow-scope reading 2:
$[A_{int}\ N\ XP_{mod}] \vDash N$
d. Hypernym reading:
$[A_{int}\ N] \vDash N'$ where $N \subseteq N'$

3 Data Collection and Discussion

There are approximately 50 intensional (sub-selective) adjectives that we have identified, from which we have selected the most frequent 30 for our investigation. Fewer than 10 of these are root adjectives (*superficial*, *putative*), and most are participial adjectival derivations, such as *alleged*, *supposed*, and *believed*. For each adjective, we have extracted 100 snippets from the corpus, where snippets are three-sentence fragments from the text. This gives us a corpus of 3,000 snippets for intensional adjectives.

We are developing an initial classification of 1,000 of these adjectives based on the inferential patterns discussed in the previous section; i.e., wide-scope, narrow-scope, and hypernym readings. These are the initial structure-to-inference templates which will constitute the small gold standard. This annotation is being performed by undergraduate linguistics majors, with three annotations per snippet. That is, we construct the examples that fit the identified test patterns, as shown in (18) and (19) below. In these examples, the inference in (18) is legitimate, while that in (19) is false.

(18) Hypernym Reading:
(T): A teenage girl has been arrested over the **alleged murder** of a mourner at a funeral in London.
(H): A mourner died.

(19) Wide-Scope Reading:
(T): She was then tried and executed in 1952 by Stalin as an **alleged spy**.
(H): She was a spy.

We then will submit these stimuli to MTurkers with the same guidelines as those given to the linguists, and examine the differences in judgments. That is, for those cases that do not accord with the pre-assigned classification, we try to isolate the factors contributing to when the judgment goes against the expected inference. To this end, we perform a statistical analysis of the contexts of the adjective for both the cases that are in accordance with the classification and the cases that are not.

The goal of this ongoing effort is to elucidate the semantic properties and inferential patterns associated with adjectives in natural language. As we have tried to make clear from this brief report, the semantic behavior of adjectives in actual language use are much more nuanced and subtle than previously documented. We hope to report on further results and insights in the near future.[4]

Acknowledgements

This research was supported by a grant from the NSF (NSF-IIS 1017765). I would like to thank Zachary Yochum, Annie Zaenen, and Christiane Fellbaum for their comments and discussion. I would also like to acknowledge the anonymous reviewers for the workshop for their helpful comments. All errors and mistakes are, of course, my own.

References

M. Amoia and C. Gardent. 2006. Adjective based inference. In *Proceedings of the Workshop KRAQ'06 on Knowledge and Reasoning for Language Processing*, pages 20–27. Association for Computational Linguistics.

M. Amoia, C. Gardent, et al. 2008. A test suite for inference involving adjectives. *Proceedings of LREC'08*, pages 19–27.

Gemma Boleda, Marco Baroni, Louise McNally, and Nghia The Pham. 2013. Intensionality was only alleged: On adjective-noun composition in distributional semantics. In *Proceedings of IWCS 2013*.

R.M.W. Dixon. 1991. *A new approach to English grammar on semantic principles*. Oxford University Press.

[4] A related paper, (Boleda et al., 2013), on the semantics of intensional adjectives, is being presented at the same venue as the present paper, and came to my attention only recently. As a result, the analysis therein has not been referenced in this paper.

H. Kamp and B. Partee. 1995. Prototype theory and compositionality. *Cognition*, pages 57–129.

H. Kamp. 1975. Two theories about adjectives. In *Formal Semantics of Natural Language*, pages 123–155. University Press.

John Lyons. 1977. *Semantics*. Cambridge University Press.

V. Raskin and S. Nirenburg. 1995. Lexical semantics of adjectives. *New Mexico State University, Computing Research Laboratory Technical Report, MCCS-95-288.*